EXCHANGE

'A tragi-comic morality tale (elegant[...]
where . . . Trifonov makes the exch[...]
examination of the fudging, the compromising, the dishonest tiny
adjustments to one's conscience made with every decision one
takes.'

Georgina Brown, *Independent*

'. . . an astonishing, painful piece of theatre, whose prevailing
notes are those of sadness and grace in the sight of domestic stress.
Yet it still manages to achieve a wry comedy of bad manners.'

Nicholas de Jongh, *Guardian*

This translation was first heard on Radio 3, and first produced
professionally for the stage at the Nuffield Theatre, Southampton,
in December 1989

YURI TRIFONOV was born in 1925 into the privileged world of
high-ranking Soviet society. His father, however, one of the Old
Bolsheviks who had joined the Party before the Revolution,
disappeared in the Stalinist purges, and his name was expunged
from Party history. Trifonov, after having won a Stalin prize for an
early novel, devoted ten years of his life to rehabilitating his
father's name. It was not until he was forty-four that he found his
true voice as a writer. There followed throughout the 1970s his
series of short novels, culminating with *Another Life* and *The House
on the Embankment*, that established him as one of the foremost
novelists of his generation. He died on 28 March 1981.

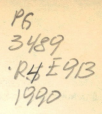

YURI TRIFONOV

EXCHANGE

Translated and introduced by
MICHAEL FRAYN

METHUEN DRAMA

METHUEN MODERN PLAY

This translation first published in 1990 by Methuen Drama, Michelin House, 81 Fulham Road, London SW3 6RB and distributed in the United States of America by HEB Inc., 70 Court Street, Portsmouth, New Hampshire 03801.

A CIP catalogue record for this book is available from the British Library.

ISBN 0-413-63440-X

Printed and bound in Great Britain by Cox & Wyman Ltd, Reading

The photograph of Yuri Trifonov on the back cover is reprinted by permission of the Novosti Press Photo Library.
The photograph on the front cover shows Martin Jarvis as *Viktor*, Marcia Warren as *Lena's Mother* and Roger Hammond as *Lena's Father* in the Nuffield Theatre, Southampton production of *Exchange*. (Photo copyright © Paul Carter)

CAUTION

INTRODUCTION

I saw the original production of *Exchange* in Moscow in 1978, and
immediately asked the author's permission to translate it; not
something I have been moved to do before or since.

It was at the Theatre on the Taganka, then in its heyday under
the direction of Yuri Lyubimov. The first breath of artistic freedom
was stirring at the Taganka, and everyone in Moscow knew it.
Lyubimov had just opened his spectacular production of *The
Master and Margarita*, adapted from Bulgakov's novel at a time
when the novel itself was still banned, and a visit to the Taganka
was a revelation of the excitement that theatre can be made to
arouse. Even as you came out of the Metro station on Taganka
Square people would be coming up to you offering to buy your
ticket. Outside the theatre itself were crowds, as for a football
match or a New York first night, being held back by *druzhinniki*,
the volunteer police auxiliaries. What were they doing here, all
those people who could never get in to see the show? Just gazing at
the good fortune of the people with tickets? Hoping one of us
would have a heart-attack and let a ticket go fluttering free in the
evening breeze?

Tickets were impossible even for *Exchange* itself, an intimate
play, austerely presented, which had already been in the repertoire
for two years. (I asked around in the interval; no one had bought
their tickets from a ticket office. They had all, in classic Soviet
style, known someone who knew someone.) It was their own lives
that people had come to see, shown as they had never been shown
in public before, in all their compromise and muddle, in all their
dogged intensity of family feeling. In fact the play remained in the
repertoire at the Taganka for another six years, until Lyubimov
was deprived of his citizenship in 1984. And when I was in
Moscow in 1988, there it was again, twelve years after its opening,
swept triumphantly back into the Taganka on the rising tide of
glasnost.

Yuri Trifonov, who wrote *Exchange*, was born in 1925, and is
increasingly recognised as one of the most outstanding of all the
fine Russian writers who have emerged since the Second World
War. He was a novelist, not a dramatist, and his only two plays,
Exchange and *The House on the Embankment*, he adapted from short

novels, under the aegis of their director, Lyubimov himself. His novels are widely read inside the Soviet Union, and for a long time now have been translated and published in Western Europe. Britain has been slow to discover them, but in 1985 Abacus issued *The House on the Embankment* and *Another Life* in translations by Michael Glenny (also available in the US as a single volume in the Touchstone imprint, published by Simon and Schuster).

Trifonov was never a dissident, but achieved the difficult feat of remaining a member of the Writers' Union (the only way in which Soviet writers can manage to publish) without losing the respect of his many disbarred and banished colleagues. He had his problems. The Taganka's production in 1980 of *The House on the Embankment*, which portrays among other things the privileges of the Soviet ruling class, was passed by the censors only after intense debate and a number of cuts. Trifonov spent ten years of his life in securing the rehabilitation of his father, an Old Bolshevik who disappeared during the purges, and *Disappearance*, the novel which he was finishing when he died in 1981, is about the shattering effect upon Russian families of first the Purges and then the war.

The world of *Exchange*, and of the other novels of his maturity, is the everyday world of Moscow, of life as it is struggled through by office workers, teachers, people clinging to the coat-tails of literature and the theatre; a world of apparently small hopes and small defeats; a world which is instantly recognisable to me through the lives of my friends in Moscow.

To an English audience one particular aspect of this world may seem rather surprisingly familiar. The confrontation of Viktor's family, with their old-fashioned revolutionary high-mindedness, and his wife's, with their down-to-earth concern for number one, may seem to reflect the clash of style that we associate with differences in class. But, in an essay replying to some of his critics, Trifonov insisted that he was not writing about the *intelligentsia* and the *meshchanstvo* (the approximate Russian equivalents of the professional and lower-middle classes). His characters were all 'the simplest and most ordinary people', and he was offering no judgments on them. He would have described them all as members of the *meshchanstvo* if the term had not acquired pejorative overtones, like *petit bourgeois*. He was writing about individuals, he said, not groups, and as a general term to describe them all, Dmitrievs and Lukyanovs alike, he suggested simply 'city-dwellers'.

This concentration upon the unheroic and the ordinary aroused the suspicions of some Soviet critics, who attacked him for '*bytovism*' – for being too concerned with *byt*. *Byt*, as Trifonov pointed out in another essay, is a word which defies translation. Marcus Wheeler's Oxford Russian-English Dictionary (one of the two best foreign language dictionaries I have ever come across) offers merely 'way of life; life'. You might wonder how a writer can be too concerned with life, and you might continue to wonder even after you had abandoned the idea of translation, and looked up the definition in the Russian equivalent of the OED: 'the general structure of life; the totality of customs and manners characteristic of any people, particular social group, etc.'

The truth, as Trifonov says in his essay, is that 'there is perhaps no more enigmatic, multi-dimensional, incomprehensible word in the Russian language'. The elucidation by example which he goes on to offer reveals a lot about his work, about Soviet and indeed Russian life, and also about one's own experience of the world. For a start, he says, *byt* 'can be something to do with the workaday and the humdrum, with the everyday domestic round, with toiling over the stove, and down to the laundry, and round the shops. The dry-cleaners, the hairdressers . . .' This, says Trifonov, is one aspect of *byt*. In Russia of course, activities such as shopping bulk particularly large, and it is no doubt *byt* in this sense that the critics are complaining Trifonov is too concerned with.

The meaning of *byt*, though, goes much wider than this. Family life, says Trifonov, is also *byt*. 'How husbands and wives get on together, and parents and children, and close and distant relations – that, too. And people being born, and old men dying, and illnesses, and weddings – that's also *byt*. And the interrelationships of friends and people at work, love, quarrels, jealousy, envy – all this, too, is *byt*.' But then, as he says, 'this is what life consists in!'.

Trifonov complains that foreign commentators on the debate about his books see *byt* as 'just one more legendary, untranslatable Russian concept . . . some special form of Russian life'. In fact, as his account makes clear, *byt* names an aspect of our own life which is only too familiar. It is life seen as a network of everyday concerns, and from this network, whatever our aspirations, we can none of us escape.

In the other essay quoted above, Trifonov describes *byt* as 'the great ordeal', the moral battlefield of modern urban man. 'It shouldn't be spoken of contemptuously, as if it were the base side of human life, unworthy of literature . . . *Byt* . . . is ordeal by life, in which the morality of today is manifested and tested.'

'We are located in a tangled and complex structure of *byt*, at the intersection of a multiplicity of connections, views, friendships, acquaintances, enmities, psychologies and ideologies. Everyone living in a big city feels daily and hourly the effect upon them of the persistent magnetic currents of this structure, which sometimes tear him to pieces. A choice has perpetually to be made, something has to be decided upon, overcome, sacrificed. You're tired? Never mind – you can rest in another place. But in this world *byt* is a war that knows no truce.'

Exchange can be seen in this way as one man's ordeal by *byt*, and this creates certain difficulties for the translator. In the first place the story of the play turns upon an aspect of *byt* in the more straightforwardly material of Trifonov's senses – the particular circumstances of Soviet housing. The text takes these for granted; every Russian in the audience has lived his entire life hedged about by them. The problem for the translator is to make certain basic facts clear to middle-class Western audience. These are:

– that the minimum permitted living-space per person in the Soviet Union is four square metres (two paces by two paces), and the maximum twelve square metres (three paces by four paces);

– that almost all Soviet housing in the cities is owned by the state, and can only be rented, never bought;

– that the only exceptions to this in the cities are the co-operatives which were introduced in the sixties, through which you can build and purchase your own flat – *if* you can find the people to do it with, and *if* you can raise the forty per cent deposit plus the mortgage repayments;

– that dachas, however, the Russian equivalent of country cottages, can be owned and let and bought and sold;

– that you might have to wait ten or twelve years to be allotted a different flat in town, so your only hope of moving is to find someone who for one reason or another is prepared to exchange with you.

But it's not just a question of the mechanism of the plot. The whole ethos of the play depends upon *byt* in the second sense – upon a precise context of place and relationships, of family customs and historical associations. It's hard enough to capture these on the page. But at least when you're reading a translation the unfamiliar syllables are spelled out before your eyes. If you don't know who Vera Zasulich was you can look her up; you can stop long enough over the saira that Lena liked so much to guess that it must at any rate be something to eat; you may not know that the Kuznetsky, where Lena's uncle sold his leather goods in the old days, was the most elegant shopping street of Tsarist Moscow, but if you've got a moment to reflect you can probably imagine its associations from the context. In the theatre, however, you've got only one chance to catch each passing syllable, and no time at all to think about it.

The sense of place in the play, its evocation of Moscow as a city, presents similar difficulties. This is one of the things that so captured my imagination when I first saw it. Moscow is a city about which I have very mixed feelings, but seen through the eyes of Trifonov's characters it seemed to become both more ordinary and more intensely real. How to convey this, though, to audiences without even a passing acquaintance with the city? Muscovites know the raw high-rises of Nagatino, where Tanya lives, and know the brilliant onion domes of the little cathedral at Kolomenskoye on which the new concrete towers look down. They know why the Agent is trying to allay people's fears of moving to Khimki-Khovrino – it's a vast housing estate rather further out of the centre of Moscow than Viktor's mother's dacha. 'Pavlinovo', the location of the dacha, is a fictitious name. But everyone familiar with Moscow would recognise it as Serebryanny bor – Silver Pinewood – an island formed by the branching of the Moscow River some twelve kilometres out to the west. It is, as Lena's mother declares, a solid and desirable neighbourhood – the British Embassy has a dacha there – and you can, as Viktor laments, see the white towers of Khimki-Khovrino in the distance across the river. His mother's dacha, incidentally, is based on a real one, which Trifonov showed me, still owned and occupied by members of his family.

Translating the play presents other difficulties, too. Trifonov wrote this version for a particular and highly idiosyncratic

production. Lyubimov's style, as anyone knows who saw his
London productions of *Crime and Punishment* and *The Possessed*, is
oblique and allusive – a comment upon the original which often
seems to assume the audience's familiarity with the text. I was
certainly very glad I had read the original story before I saw the
production of *Exchange* at the Taganka. And even this is difficult
to reconstruct from the published text, which was intended for
people who knew what they were doing anyway, and contains only
the most sparse and cryptic stage-directions. There are some plays,
of course, which need few stage-directions. This is not one of
them. In his stories Trifonov distances the action by presenting it
through fragmented layers of memory, and the theatrical equivalent
for this which he and Lyubimov devised involves a similar
complexity.

All in all, it seemed to me that the play needed not just
translating but a good deal of rethinking to make it workable on a
British stage. After I had done a first draft I went back to Moscow
and got Trifonov's consent to various changes. In the first place I
decided to introduce stage-directions that would suggest a rather
different style of production from Lyubimov's. The original staging
was austere and abstract. So far as I recall, most of the cast
remained on for most of the evening, sitting in a line across the
stage in front of a heap of assorted *bric-à-brac*. I felt that a
production outside Russia would have to make the physical
locations more tangible. It would have to offer us some suggestion
of the dacha in Pavlinovo and the co-operative flat in Nagatino.
Above all, it would have to make physically clear why it was so
imperative for the Dmitrievs to move, by establishing the reality of
life in a space of eighteen square metres.

I also adapted the text to make clear how an exchange of flats
worked, and I got Trifonov's permission to restore various sections
from the original novel – mostly ones that helped to bring alive the
physical reality of Moscow, and fleshed out the lives of his
characters. I expanded allusions and simplified details (saira became
tinned salmon, for instance). When my version was finished,
Trifonov had it read by a translator friend in Moscow and
approved it.

That was in 1979. Since then the translation has been performed
on BBC Radio 3, and by drama students at the Guildhall School in

London. It has also been given a rehearsed reading to an audience in Chicago, who were reported to be largely uncomprehending. But getting a professional stage production for it has taken ten whole years. I feel rather uneasy that during this time I have made use of at least one of the techniques I learnt from the play – direct narration interspersed with remembered scenes. I think I first saw this in Peter Nichols's *Forget-Me-Not Lane*, back in 1971. But in translating *Exchange* I had the technique in my own hands, so to speak, and it remained there when I came to write *Benefactors*.

When at last Patrick Sandford announced that he would produce it at the Nuffield Theatre in Southampton I decided to celebrate by writing a fresh draft. Seeing it at the Guildhall and hearing of the incomprehension in Chicago have persuaded me to make the action clearer still. I have divided it into two acts, which has meant a certain rearrangement of events at the end of Act One, and cut some of the minor characters. Since I did the earlier version I have translated five more plays from the Russian (and seen them produced), and in the process have found out a little more about how to do it, which has encouraged me to be rather bolder with the dialogue. I hope all my changes have remained faithful to the spirit of the original. But this time Trifonov is no longer there to consult.

Whatever the translator does, of course, the play can never have the same familiarity to an English audience that it does to a Russian one. But this has some advantages. It has the effect of showing us our own world at a distance, the too familiar tangle of our own existence made new and unfamiliar by being refracted through someone else's *byt*. Because in the end this is us. In these cramped and gimcrack rooms, in these unfamiliar suburbs, we are watching our own small wars, our own small victories and defeats. The little adjustments of the conscience that Viktor makes are the ones we all make, and the cumulative effects they have on him they will have on us, too. And as we see his life slip through his fingers, never fully grasped or properly understood, we for a moment catch a brief hold upon our own.

MICHAEL FRAYN

This translation of *Exchange* was given its first professional stage performance at the Nuffield Theatre, Southampton, on 21 November 1989, with the following cast:

VIKTOR	Martin Jarvis
LENA	Rosalind Ayres
VIKTOR'S MOTHER	Faith Brooke
VIKTOR'S FATHER	John Hudson
VIKTOR'S GRANDFATHER	Colin Douglas
LORA	Gabrielle Lloyd
FELIX/SNITKIN	Richard Clews
LENA'S FATHER	Roger Hammond
LENA'S MOTHER	Marcia Warren
ZHEREKHOV/KALUGIN/ LYOVKA BUBRIK	James Snell
AUNT ZHENYA/DIRECTOR	Jean Rimmer
TANYA/COUSIN MARINA	Lavinia Bertram
AGENT	John Baddeley

Directed by Patrick Sandford
Designed by Tanya McCallin
Lighting by Jenny Cane

ACT ONE

Moscow, with its streets and offices, its housing estates and its rural outskirts; and, in one small corner of the city, the Dmitrievs' flat.

The flat is a tiny single room, crammed with furniture, where all three members of the family live, eat, and sleep. When the double divan is unfolded to make a a bed there is no room to sit at the table.

The rest of the stage is empty, and can be simply furnished with a table and chairs, to represent all the other settings in the play.

People on the streets. From among them VIKTOR *emerges and comes towards us.*

VIKTOR (*to audience*). Fear. That was the first thing I felt. Not anger. The anger came later. That and many other things . . . Now it's all over I'm trying to understand it. I'm trying to make sense of all these things that have piled up in my life. Trying to work out what my crime actually was.

> LENA *enters, and sits down at the dining-table. She works on books and papers in a space made by pushing back the tablecloth and the items that remain on the table from one meal to the next.*

VIKTOR. It was late one evening when Lena first brought the subject up. This was in October, just after my mother came out of hospital. And it wasn't anger that I felt first of all. We couldn't have a row, in any case – Natashka was still up, still working.

> NATASHKA *emerges from behind a screen in the flat, and fetches a ruler from the table.*

LENA. Natashka! Come on. We all want to go to bed.

NATASHKA. Just a moment.

She disappears behind the screen again.

VIKTOR. She'd got her own little room, really, behind there. Bed. Her own desk. I'd fixed up a light for her, and shelves for her books. 'Where's Natashka?' we used to say. 'In solitary.'

NATASHKA *emerges from behind the screen, holding exercise book and textbook.*

NATASHKA (*to* LENA). Specific heat. Is that kilocalories? Or do you leave the kilocalories out?

LENA. You must stop now. It's after ten.

She looks at NATASHKA's books, trying to help her.

VIKTOR. When she was a little girl we had a nanny sleeping in here as well, on a folding bed. We tried putting her in the hall, but the Fandeyevs objected. They're the people in the next room, the people we share the flat with. So she had to come in here. Poor old soul, she suffered from a combination of insomnia and very acute hearing. All night long she'd be muttering and grunting and listening. If it wasn't a mouse scratching, it would be a cockroach running, or a tap someone had forgotten to turn off in the kitchen. It was like a second honeymoon for Lena and me when she went.

NATASHKA. I've still got maths to do.

She goes back behind the screen.

VIKTOR. A communal flat. That's the point. One room, plus kitchen and bathroom shared with the next-door neighbours. Eighteen square metres. Five paces long by four paces wide.

LENA. *I'm* going to bed, anyway.

She drags the table aside.

I hear the Markusheviches are looking for an exchange.

VIKTOR. And that was the first time the word was mentioned. I hardly noticed it. We were getting the bed out at the time.

He helps LENA *to fold out the double divan and make it up.*

LENA. They're separating, apparently.

VIKTOR. Who are?

LENA. The Markusheviches.

VIKTOR. Do I know them?

LENA. Irina's friends.

VIKTOR. Made in Czechoslovakia, our bed. The envy of all our friends when we bought it, three years ago.

LENA. So now they're looking for separate flats.

VIKTOR. What have they got?

LENA. Two rooms. Self-contained. On Malaya Gruzinskaya.

VIKTOR. Rather rickety now. Squeaks with every move.

LENA. I thought if we offered them this flat, together with your mother's, they might be interested.

VIKTOR. My mother's flat?

LENA. It's just round the corner from where his wife works. And it's a nice room – it's twenty square metres. You've always wanted your mother to live with us – she's always dreamed of living with you. Now she's out of hospital she's going to need looking after more and more. And if we had an extra room . . .

VIKTOR. An extra room . . . I saw at once the simple secret thought in Lena's mind. And the first thing I felt was fear.

LENA *and* NATASHKA *go off.*

VIKTOR. So this was how it would end. A story that had been going on all these years. How did it start?

The lights come up on another part of the set – a dacha, in the pinewoods by the Moscow River.

Enter LORA.

LORA. Vitka!

She sits on the edge of the table, fanning herself with a newspaper.

VIKTOR. It started with a nail. A nail and a bucket.

LORA. Vitka, I want a word with you.

VIKTOR. This was when we were first married. We were living with my mother. Not in her one-room flat in town, of course. In the little dacha she had out at Pavlinovo. We'd nowhere else. Occasionally my sister Lora would come and stay. She wasn't living in the dacha then – this was when her tedious romance with Felix was only just beginning.

LORA. I'd like to have a little talk about Lena, if I may. Nothing special – don't get alarmed. Just silly little things. You know how much I like her. Anyway the main thing as far as I'm concerned is that you love her.

VIKTOR. An opening that immediately offended me. Because the main thing wasn't that at all. The main thing was that she was wonderful quite regardless of me.

Crosses to LORA.

VIKTOR. Go on.

LORA. I'm just a bit taken aback by one or two things. Mother would never dream of saying anything herself, but I can see what she's thinking . . . You won't be offended, now, will you, Vitka?

VIKTOR. Oh, honestly! What is it?

LORA. Well, this really is very silly. It's simply that Lena has – well, for example, she's commandeered all our best cups. It's just that she always puts the slop-bucket outside the door to Mama's room . . .

VIKTOR (*to the audience*). My God! And it's Lora saying this! My dear sister! The archeologist! (*To* LORA.) I hadn't noticed. I'll tell her, though.

LORA. No, no, no. It's dreadful my coming to you with all this nonsense. But I've been telling Mama off about it. Why doesn't she just say: 'Lena dear, we need the cups back, and please, don't put the bucket here – put it over there instead.' In fact I said as much today, and I don't think she took it amiss. Though I hate mentioning tiny points like this, believe me. But there's something else that did rather grate on me.

For some reason she's removed that picture of Papa from the middle room and hung it in the hallway. Mama was very taken aback. This is something you really have to know about, because it's not just another little domestic detail – it's something else altogether. If you want my opinion, it shows a certain lack of regard for other people's feelings.

VIKTOR. Oh, come on! I'll speak to her about the picture. But listen, supposing you happened to be in someone else's house. Mightn't you tread on a few toes?

LORA. Possibly. But not like that.

Enter LENA *in the dacha.*

LORA (*to the audience*). I took that picture down purely and simply because I wanted the nail to fix the clock on, and that's absolutely all there was to it.

Enter LENA'S MOTHER *in the dacha, followed by* LENA's FATHER.

LENA'S MOTHER. Lena!

LENA'S FATHER (*to his wife*). Vera!

LORA. Mama, don't *you* start!

Her parents sit down in two chairs – guests waiting to be enter- tained, anxious not to have a family quarrel in someone else's house

VIKTOR. Her parents had moved in – temporarily, just for August and September – just to help out, because Lena was expecting the baby. They were sleeping in the middle room. My mother was in the little red room. So was Lora, on the few occasions when she came to stay. We were on the glassed-in verandah.

LENA'S MOTHER (*to the audience*). My husband had the whole place redecorated for them. The floors done. New wallpaper. They couldn't have lived here as it was.

LENA. I do think it's a little peculiar, I must say, when it's such a tiny thing, that your mother didn't come and speak to me herself, instead of sending you as an ambassador, which blows it up into something out of all proportion.

VIKTOR. Mama hasn't breathed a word.

LENA. So who did?

VIKTOR. Whereupon I had to go and let out that it was Lora. How many more things were going to be stupidly let out after that!

Enter VIKTOR'S MOTHER *in the dacha, carrying the tea things, which she places on the table. This is what* LENA'S PARENTS *have been waiting for. They make appreciative noises.*

VIKTOR. Marvellous, when you look back on it! Was it ever really like this? – Everyone sitting together on the verandah at the big table, drinking tea. Mama pouring. My mother-in-law cutting the fruit tart. There was even a time when she used to call Lora . . .

LENA'S MOTHER. Lorochka.

VIKTOR. Lorochka. And she took her to her own favourite dressmakers . . .

LENA'S MOTHER. Yes, I did.

VIKTOR. That's how it was. Wasn't it? It was, it was. Only it hasn't stayed in the memory – it's gone, vanished.

The lights on the dacha go down, but remain up on VIKTOR *and* LENA.

Because I couldn't live by anything except Lena, couldn't see anyone but Lena. There was the south – stifling – the Black Sea coast in the heat of summer – and the old lady I rented the room from, next to the bazaar – and some man I had a fight with over Lena on the waterfront at night – he'd been trying to slip her a note in the restaurant. And us with no money, wiring home, living on nothing but cucumbers – and Lena lying on the bed, helpless, naked, black against the sheets – and me running out to sell the camera. And after we'd come back it all went on still, even though things were different. Moscow, and I'd started work. We were living at the dacha. One wild summer flew by. And again Lena lay dark as a mulatto against the sheets – and again there was swimming until it was almost dark, and races across the river; the meadows growing cool; conversations; revelations; tireless and supple bodies; fingers ashamed of nothing; lips always ready for love. 'Look, Mama – what a sense of style Lena's got! We've lived here for all these years, and we've never thought of hanging that mat on the wall! The whole place has been transformed! No, she's got really subtle taste. Not like you and me!' There was no one with a skin as soft as Lena's; no one who knew how to love me as Lena did. I was living stunned and stupefied, the way you do in the heat when you can't think and you languish half-asleep behind drawn curtains.

Exit LENA. *The lights come up on the dacha.* LENA's *parents,* VICTOR'S MOTHER, *and* LORA *are sitting as before, but are all stiff and constrained.*

When I came back from town, the day after my talk with Lora about the nail and the bucket, it was strangely quiet in the dacha.

LORA. I'd left for Moscow.

Exit LORA.

VIKTOR'S MOTHER. I'd been staying in my room.

LENA'S MOTHER. My husband and I are most grateful for all your hospitality, and we are just waiting for the taxi that my husband has called.

VIKTOR'S MOTHER. Do come and see us again.

LENA'S MOTHER. I doubt if we shall be able to manage it. Such a lot of things we have to do. And so many friends wanting to see us, all inviting us to their dachas.

LENA's *parents move away from the dacha, then wait, on their dignity. Exit* VIKTOR'S MOTHER.

VIKTOR. The picture of Father was back in its old place.

Enter LENA.

LENA. Your sister seems to have taken it upon herself to pass remarks about me. If she's not doing it to my face she's doing it behind my back. Do you want me to hot up your dinner?

Exit LENA.

VIKTOR. Mama . . . ?

Enter VIKTOR'S MOTHER.

VIKTOR'S MOTHER. Vitka, I'm very put out. I can't get to sleep for thinking of it.

VIKTOR. Thinking of what?

VIKTOR'S MOTHER. Their going off like that.

VIKTOR. Oh, mother, it's such a nonsense! It's not worth talking about.

VIKTOR'S MOTHER. Yes, but Lora should have controlled herself. Why did she have to start all that? And you went and told Lena about the nail – it's all so absurd – and she told her mother. We had a most idiotic talk about it . . . Such utter nonsense!

VIKTOR. And all because people shouldn't go moving the family portraits around! Anyway, they've gone, so that's all right. Lena said absolutely nothing to me about it, not a word. She's no fool. So don't get worked up about it. Sleep well.

Exit VIKTOR'S MOTHER.

Enter LENA.

LENA. What were you talking to your mother about?

VIKTOR. Don't you start. I'm tired.

LENA. We're very proud people, Vitka. How could you do such a thing? My mother's particularly proud and sensitive. The point being that she has never in all her life been dependent upon anyone.

VIKTOR (*to the audience*). Not dependent? How not dependent, when she's never worked – when she's always lived off her husband?

LENA'S FATHER. Yes.

LENA'S MOTHER. Yes.

VIKTOR (*to* LENA). How have we impugned her independence?

LENA'S MOTHER. They surely can't think we're trying to lay claim to any of their rooms?

VIKTOR. What's all this about laying claim?

LENA. You're going to ring Mama from work tomorrow, though, and very gently, very tactfully – not mentioning the picture or any grievances – you're going to invite them back to Pavlinovo. They won't come, of course, because they're very proud people . . .

VIKTOR (*to the audience*). I rang. They arrived the following day.

LENA'S PARENTS *cross back to the dacha.*

LENA'S FATHER. Hello!

LENA'S MOTHER. Hello!

Enter VIKTOR'S MOTHER.

LENA'S FATHER. A cake!

LENA'S MOTHER. It's a chocolate log

LENA'*s parents resume their places at the table.* LENA *joins them.* VIKTOR'S MOTHER *pours tea for them.*

VIKTOR. What made me think of that ancient business? Later on there were a lot of things worse than that. We even came to blows.

LENA'S FATHER. The cheeky blighter.

VIKTOR. But – probably because it was the first time – it imprinted itself on me forever. I can even remember the overcoat her mother was wearing.

LENA'S MOTHER. Good heavens above, which one was it? Oh, the one with the cape top.

VIKTOR. There was a time when it all made my life a misery. Because of my mother I kept having these terrible skirmishes with Lena.

LENA. Control yourself, will you, Vitya.

VIKTOR. I'd fly into a wild rage at the slightest word, if it came from Lena. And because of my wife I'd be let in for painful discussions – 'just to get things clear' – with my mother.

VIKTOR'S MOTHER. Vitya!

Enter LORA.

LORA. Mama!

VIKTOR. After which my mother wouldn't speak to me for several days. I obstinately struggled to bring them together, to reconcile them. I installed them together at the dacha. Once I booked them both seaside holidays in Riga.

LENA'S MOTHER. Oh, Mr Hercules!

VIKTOR. But none of it came to anything. Between those two women stood some kind of barrier, and to overcome it was quite beyond them. Why it should have been thus I never understood, though I often pondered it. Why should two educated women, respected by all who knew them – my mother was senior librarian in one of the big academic libraries – Lena was an English technical translator, and everyone said an outstandingly good one – why should two good women, both of them passionately devoted to me – also a reasonably decent man – and to my daughter Natashka – why should they nourish this mutual antipathy that only grew stronger over the years? I agonized, I beat my brains – and then I got used to it. I got used to it because I'd observed that it was the same with everyone – and everyone got used to it.

LENA'S FATHER. Yes.

LENA'S MOTHER. Yes.

LORA. Yes.

VIKTOR'S MOTHER. Yes.

Exit VICTOR'S MOTHER, LORA, *and* LENA's *parents, taking the tea things with them. The lights go down, leaving only* VIKTOR *illuminated.*

An ambulance siren. It dies away in the distance.

VIKTOR. Last July my mother became seriously ill and they took her into hospital. She was in for twelve days, and they suspected the worst. In October they operated on her, and the worst was confirmed.

The lights come up again on the dacha. Grey October. Enter VIKTOR'S MOTHER *slowly, followed by* LORA.

VIKTOR'S MOTHER. I'm so glad I'm going to be home for the holidays! I feel quite well again!

VIKTOR. You're looking much better.

LORA *nods but says nothing.*

VIKTOR'S MOTHER. No, I really am being a good girl! I've put on weight . . .

She sits down. LORA *looks after her.*

VIKTOR. And it was at precisely that moment, when my mother came out of hospital, that Lena started on the exchange. Our one-roomed flat. My mother's one-room flat. We'd put them up for exchange and we'd get a two-room flat where we could all live together. All four of us, until my mother . . . until my mother didn't need the room any more. Yes, I saw at once the simple secret thought in Lena's mind, and my heart was touched by fear.

The lights come up on the flat. Enter LENA *in a dressing gown. She begins to prepare for bed.* VIKTOR *crosses to the flat, and begins to take off his shoes and tie.*

LENA. It's our one and only chance – and it won't come again! Look, we might be on the housing list for ten years or more before they give us a bigger flat! It's not as if we were exchanging the dacha! We're not talking about her precious dacha! Our flat – and your mother's flat in town! They'll like your mother's room, no doubt about that, but I expect they'll want cash to make up the value of ours. They won't be interested otherwise. Of course, we could try to exchange our room for something more worthwhile first, make it a three-way exchange. Nothing frightening about that. We just have to put our backs into it. Get something done each day. The best thing would be to find an agent. Luda's got a little man she knows. Very nice old boy. Of course, he won't give anyone his address or phone number.

Enter AGENT, *hurrying across the stage.*

AGENT (*to the audience*). Would you, if you were in my shoes?

LENA. He just suddenly appears out the blue.

AGENT. And get that light off me!

Exit AGENT.

LENA. All very cloak and dagger, but he should be showing up at Luda's before too long because she owes him money.

VIKTOR. It was strange. I felt neither anger nor pain. Only – fleetingly – something about the pitilessness of life.

LENA. Because that's an absolute rule – never pay any money in advance . . .

LORA. Lena was always distinguished by a certain moral – not blindness, that's too strong – but by a certain fuzziness of moral vision . . . And after all, you can't really be angry with someone because they happen to be tone-deaf, say.

Exit LORA.

VIKTOR'S MOTHER. But Lena has another quality, and a very powerful one it is – the ability to get her own way!

Enter LENA'S MOTHER.

LENA'S MOTHER. Yes, she does. She does.

Exit LENA'S MOTHER.

VIKTOR. Where does Lena come into all this? She's merely a part of life, a part of its harshness. (*To* LENA.) What do we need an agent for, if you've already found another flat?

LENA. We need an agent if we're going to have to swap our place first. And to speed things up generally. I shan't pay him a kopeck until I've got the authorization from the housing department in my hand. It won't cost all that much. A hundred roubles. A hundred and fifty at most.

VIKTOR (*calls, softly*). Natash.

LENA. It's all right, she's asleep.

VIKTOR. It might have been better if you'd waited to see if I brought the subject up first. And if I didn't then that was because it was wrong, it was out of bounds, it was something we shouldn't have been thinking about now.

LENA. I know, Vitya, I know. I'm sorry. But . . . well, in the first place, you *have* already brought the subject up, haven't you. Many, many times. And then again this is something we all need – and your mother most of all. Vitya, love, I know what you mean, and I feel for you most terribly, and I'm telling you – we need it! Do trust me . . .

VIKTOR. You shouldn't have brought it up now!

LENA. Well, all right, I'm sorry. But, listen, I'm not worrying about myself, truly I'm not . . .

VIKTOR (*in a whisper*). Voice down!

LENA. You seem to be accusing me of having no feelings, but honestly and truly, Vitya, I was thinking about all of us. I was thinking about Natasha's future . . .

VIKTOR. How *can* you? How can you *do* it?

LENA. Do what?

VIKTOR. How can you talk about a thing like that now? How can you actually utter the words? That's what amazes me. God in heaven, there's some moral defect in you. Some stunting of the feelings. Something – forgive me – but something *not quite human*. How could you? The point being that it's *my* mother who's ill, not yours! Right? And if I were in your place . . .

LENA. Not so loud . . .

VIKTOR. If I were in your place I'd never been the first to suggest it . . .

LENA. Sh!

Pause. LENA *gets into bed.*

Natashka was sitting up with her physics until eleven o'clock again. We'll have to find someone . . . Antonina Alekseyevna's got hold of a good coach.

VIKTOR *undresses.*

VIKTOR. The fact that Lena had turned the conversation on to Natashka's difficulties, and put up with all my insults – just let them go straight over her head – which wasn't like her – meant that she very much wanted to make up and declare the matter closed. But I didn't feel like making up yet. On the contrary; my irritation was growing because I'd suddenly realised what Lena's main offence was: that she'd spoken as if everything had already been decided – as if it was perfectly clear to me as well that everything had already been decided – as if we understood each other without the need for words. She'd spoken as if there were no hope. She had a nerve . . . Now she was content; the hardest part had been done; she had said it.

VIKTOR *gets into bed and lies with his back to her.*

Now all that had to be done was to lick the wound. And indeed it wasn't even a wound – it was a slight scratch. A slight scratch which it had been absolutely necessary to inflict. A sort of injection. Just hold the cotton-wool. It'll hurt a bit, but it'll be all right afterwards. The important thing, of course, was that *afterwards* it would be all right. And I hadn't cried out – I hadn't drummed my feet on the floor.

LENA *puts her hand on his shoulder.*

That's not a caress. It's a gesture of friendship – perhaps even a honest confession of guilt. A plea to turn over and face her.

LENA'*s hand has begun to stroke his shoulder.*

She felt sorry for me; she was excusing the hardness of her

heart – for which, however, justification could be found; she was summoning me to wiser and kindlier counsels, so that I too should find strength within myself, and take pity on her.

The lights in the flat fade to illuminate only VIKTOR *and* LENA *in bed.*

Something unappeased in me prevented me from turning over. Through my gathering drowsiness I saw the porch of that little wooden house in Pavlinovo, and Mama standing on the topmost step, on that icy spring day before we were married.

Enter VIKTOR'S MOTHER *at the dacha.*

VIKTOR'S MOTHER. Have you thought carefully, my son?

VIKTOR. God in heaven! That was Mama's misfortune – to say straight out whatever came into her head . . . 'Have you thought carefully, my son?' Could anything have less force than those absurd, pathetic words?

LENA. Never before . . . not with anyone . . for as long as I live . . .

VIKTOR'S MOTHER. Vitya, get up! Time for our English lesson!

LENA (*whispers*). We're asleep, we're asleep, we're asleep . . .

VIKTOR. We're asleep, we're asleep . . .

Exit VIKTOR'S MOTHER.

And it was there, on that verandah where we slept, that everything started. All the things that can now never be put right. In fourteen years that hand has changed, too.

LENA. Say something, then! Why won't you say anything?

Darkness in the flat. Then brisk morning music on the radio, and full lighting in the flat.

VIKTOR *and* LENA *get up.* VIKTOR *pulls on his trousers. Exit* LENA, *banging on* NATASHKA's *screen as she goes.*

Enter NATASHKA *from behind screen, dressed, searching for stuff to put in satchel.*

Enter LENA'S MOTHER. *She ties* NATASHKA's *braids.*

Sound of toilet flushing. Enter LENA *hurriedly.*

Exit VIKTOR *hurriedly. Everyone gets in everyone else's way, but it is plain that they are used to it.*

LENA *and her* MOTHER *fold away the bed.* NATASHKA *pulls out the dining-table. Sound of toilet flushing.*

Enter VIKTOR *with a towel round his neck, cleaning his teeth.*

Exit LENA. *The music ends.*

VIKTOR (*to the audience*). I'd been thirty-seven in August. I sometimes thought that everything was still in front of me.

LENA'S MOTHER. Yes.

VIKTOR. These bouts of optimism would usually occur in the morning, when I'd woken up suddenly fresh, and unexpectedly cheerful. The weather had a lot to do with it.

Enter LENA *left carrying breakfast things.*

NATASHKA. Porridge again! Haven't you any imagination?

LENA. I'll give you imagination! Sit up properly!

LENA'S MOTHER. If other children had your advantages . . .

VIKTOR. This was downright dishonest. Other children all had as much and more besides.

Examines himself in the mirror, and feels the smoothness of his cheeks.

Thirty-seven. That's not forty-seven, and it's not fifty-seven. I still might get somewhere.

The sound of someone banging on the door.

WOMAN NEXT DOOR (*off*). *Please* hurry up in there! It's Friday – I've got all my washing to do!

VIKTOR. Right. All yours.

VIKTOR *takes one last look at his face in the mirror, then goes to the telephone in the flat and dials.*

LENA'S MOTHER. He was very quick out of the bathroom this morning. Full marks there. Next door must have been on at him.

LENA. What's next door got to do with it? Vitya's always quick in the bathroom.

LENA'S MOTHER. I'm saying – full marks! That's the style!

Enter VIKTOR'S MOTHER. *She picks up another telephone.*

VIKTOR'S MOTHER (*into phone*). Hello?

VIKTOR (*into phone*). That you, Mama? How are things?

VIKTOR'S MOTHER. The doctor looked in late last night. He said I was getting on very well. My blood-pressure's normal. He wants me to go into a sanatorium somewhere outside Moscow as soon as the first snow falls.

VIKTOR. Good, Mama! That's very good!

VIKTOR'S MOTHER. How's my Natashka getting on? You are giving her carrots, aren't you?

VIKTOR. Hold on.

LENA. We are.

VIKTOR (*into phone*). Yes.

VIKTOR'S MOTHER. Has she done the corrections for that 'C' she got in physics?

LENA. She has.

NATASHKA. Yes.

VIKTOR. Yes, she has.

GIRL NEXT DOOR (*off*). Natashka!

LENA'S MOTHER. There's Valya.

NATASHKA *finishes a last mouthful, and runs off, being kissed by* LENA.

LENA (*calls after her*). Have you both got your satchels?

LENA'S MOTHER *goes off to see.*

LENA. And don't run across the road!

VIKTOR. All right, Mama. I'll try and look in this evening.

> VIKTOR *puts the phone down.*

> *Exit* HIS MOTHER.

VIKTOR (*to the audience*). And suddenly it seemed as if the whole thing might just sort itself out. Mistakes do happen.

> *He pats* LENA *playfully on the bottom.*

What kind of mood are you in today, then?

LENA. A bad mood.

VIKTOR. Why? What's wrong?

> VIKTOR *and* LENA *get dressed.*

LENA. Plenty of things. Mama's ill.

> *Enter* LENA's *parents.*

LENA'S FATHER. The chemist's? I'll pop down there straight away. What's our woman called?

VIKTOR. Your mother?

LENA. You think yours is the only one who might be ill? You could see when she came this morning – she's far from well.

VIKTOR. What's the matter with her?

LENA. Something with her head. Some kind of violent pains. Her blood-pressure's gone way up.

VIKTOR (*to the audience*). I'll lay you a hundred to one it's just her usual migraine.

LENA'S MOTHER (*sarcastic*). Oh, it's nothing at all!

LENA'S FATHER. The cheeky blighter!

> *Exit* LENA's *parents up right.* VIKTOR *sits down at the breakfast table.*

LENA. Oh, and Vitya, don't forget to say thank you to Mama. She did come and get you breakfast this morning in spite of being ill.

VIKTOR. Lena could perfectly well have got me breakfast herself, but she used to entrust this task to her mother so that not for a moment should I forget how much I owed her.

LENA. Vitya, if you're going to Pavlinovo today, please remember to get the key off your mother.

VIKTOR. I'm not sure I'll be going.

LENA. But you said to her on the phone, didn't you? The Markushevices can be looking at her flat, and we must have the key.

VIKTOR. When do they want to look at it?

LENA. Tomorrow or the day after. I don't know exactly. They're going to ring. So don't forget the key. Put the yoghurt in the fridge, will you, and the bread in its bag. You keep leaving it out, and it goes dry. 'Bye, then.

Exit LENA.

VIKTOR (*to the audience*). The doctor's right. He knows his job – he's an old hand at this game. We've got to get mother into the sanatorium. It may just be that everything will sort itself out. It'll work as psychotherapy, too – mental healing. We'll do the exchange, we'll get a nice self-contained flat with two rooms, and we'll all live together. And the sooner we do it the better. For mother's sake. Her dream come true.

He gets up and begins to clear the breakfast things, taking them off as he talks.

No, Lena can sometimes be very wise – intuitively wise, womanly wise. Because this may be a stroke of genius, the only possible way to save a life. When the surgeons are powerless other forces come into play. And this is something that no professor can do for her – that no one else can do for her – no one at all . . . So who wants a nice flat in central Moscow? Who wants two nice flats . . . ?

Exit VIKTOR, carrying his briefcase.

An office. The clatter of typewriters.

ZHEREKHOV *enters the office with files and papers, which he lays out on the table.*

Enter the DIRECTOR OF THE INSTITUTE.
ZHEREKHOV *takes her umbrella and hangs it up for her. She sits down at the table, and looks at the papers which* ZHEREKHOV *has laid out.*

VIKTOR *enters the office. The* DIRECTOR *indicates the chair in front of her desk, and continues to look at her papers.* VIKTOR *sits down.*

VIKTOR (*to the audience*). In the office that day the decision was being taken about who had to go out to Siberia on the Golyshmanovo job. We supply machinery to the oil and gas industry. The trip had been finalised back in July, and the man who was supposed to be going was me.

DIRECTOR. So what are we going to do?

VIKTOR. I don't know. I can't go.

SNITKIN *strolls into the office, and perches on the edge of the* DIRECTOR'*s desk.*

VIKTOR (*to the audience*). The week before I'd got talking to Pasha Snitkin, a rather sharp operator in the department. Not one job did he ever do off his own bat – he always fixed it so that everyone had to help him out.

SNITKIN (*to* VIKTOR). Listen, old son, I can't go. Can't possibly do it, comrades. Unfortunately. Same thing – family circumstances.

VIKTOR. He was probably lying. But with something like this he had a right to. Who wants to go out to Siberia, in the cold and wet?

Enter AGENT, *hurrying across the stage.*

AGENT. You can see his point.

Exit AGENT.

SNITKIN. Anyway, I thought you said your mother was better?

VIKTOR. How can she be better? (*To the audience.*) The thing
was that Pasha had always asked so attentively after my
mother's health – he'd been so full of sympathy all round –
that I'd somehow been absolutely sure he'd agree. But why
should he? It's not that people are being hypocritical when
they show sympathy, when they ask you with real heartfelt
concern: 'So – how are things at home?' It's just that this
sympathy, this real heartfelt concern, comes in a particular
size, like shoes or hats. It mustn't be stretched too far. Pasha
Snitkin was getting his little girl into music school, and the
only one who could handle this ticklish business was himself.
Her mother – her grandmother – they wouldn't do – it had to
be him. And if he had to be away in November, then music
school this year would certainly go by the board, which would
be a terrible trauma for the girl, and a moral blow to the
whole Snitkin family.

SNITKIN. Yes, it would.

VIKTOR. But, good God, can you really compare them – someone
dying and a girl starting music school? Oh yes. Yes, you can.
They're hats of roughly the same size – if it's a member of
someone else's family who's dying, and your own dear
daughter who's starting music school.

SNITKIN. Yes, it is.

ZHEREKHOV (*thoughtfully*). Yes.

DIRECTOR (*likewise*). Yes . . . So how are we going to do it?
Um? Supposing we said just for ten days or so?

VIKTOR. No. (*To the audience.*) I'd realised that I could stand like
a rock and not be shifted. All it needed was not to explain
anything.

DIRECTOR. All right. Tyagusov can go.

VIKTOR. Tyagusov. Of course. I'll sit in with him for a couple of
days and explain everything. He'll manage. He's got his head
screwed on the right way. (*To the audience.*) Pretty much of a
halfwit, in fact – he's only just out of college. In the past –
and not so long ago, either – I'd have raised some protest. But

now I suddenly felt that the whole thing was meaningless. Why not Tyagusov? Now all I had to do was to borrow some money. For the doctor alone it was costing – four fifteens – sixty rubles a month. Who could I touch for it? Practically everyone had been complaining recently that money was tight.

The DIRECTOR *and* ZHEREKHOV *continue to work.*
SNITKIN *wanders off right, leafing through a magazine.*

VIKTOR. Like everyone who's oppressed by fate I'd become superstitious. I couldn't help noticing that there are lucky days when one success comes riding on the coat-tails of another, and on days like these you had to pack in as many things as possible. There are also unlucky days when nothing goes right, however hard you try.

Enter LENA. *She picks up a phone.*

VIKTOR. It looked as if one of the good days was beginning. How to tell my mother about the exchange, though? She knew perfectly well, of course, what Lena thought about her living with us – and now here was Lena actually suggesting it. Why?

The office phone rings. VIKTOR *picks it up.*

(*Into the phone.*) Construction 4.

LENA (*into phone*). Dmitriev, please.

VIKTOR. It's me.

LENA. So what, Vitya, you don't want to tell her?

VIKTOR. I don't know how to. Couldn't I just say it's one possible idea . . . ? Do you see what I mean?

LENA. Put it like this. Say that you're very keen to do it, and that I'm against it. But you insisted. In other words, you're doing it in spite of me, right? Then it'll all seem perfectly natural, and your mother won't think twice about it. Put all the blame on to me. Only don't overdo it. Just a hint or two . . . Right – bye, then. Oh, Vitya, Vitya! Have a talk to someone at work who's done a successful exchange, yes? 'Bye.

Exit LENA.

Enter TANYA *in another part of the office.*

VIKTOR. What Lena was saying was of course perfectly right and very shrewd. The only thing I could think to do was to go and see Tanya about it.

TANYA. What?

VIKTOR. No, no – nothing bad. Perhaps even a bit better than before. Tan, do you know, has anyone in the department done an exchange? An exchange of flats?

TANYA. I don't know. I think perhaps Zherekhov. Why?

VIKTOR. I need some advice. We've got to do an exchange rather urgently, you see.

TANYA. You and Lena? Both of you?

VIKTOR. Yes.

TANYA. You want to . . . find somewhere to live with your mother?

VIKTOR. Yes, yes! It's absolutely vital. Take too long to explain, but it just has to be done at once.

Enter LENA. *She listens to what she already knows.*

(*To the audience.*) Three years back all this had started; lasted all one summer; and then ended of its own accord, when Lena and Natashka came back from holiday. Or rather, it didn't end – it dragged thinly on. It broke up over the course of six months or so. I knew that from any reasonable point of view she would have been the better wife for me.

LENA. There you're wrong, my dear.

VIKTOR. No, but being reasonable, looking at it reasonably . . .

LENA *smiles, and goes off.*

Tanya had a husband and a son. The husband loved Tanya very much, and forgave her everything. But after that summer three years before she no longer wanted to live with him, and they separated. The husband became an unhappy man. He gave up his job, he went away from Moscow. Tanya wanted to leave the office, too, so as not to see me every day, but leaving turned out to be difficult. Then gradually she came to terms with it all, and we learnt to meet calmly and talk like old friends. Now I've told her about the exchange she's thinking: so that's it – never. (*To* TANYA.) What can I do, though? This is some kind of chance, do you see, some kind of hope. And of course my mother's always dreamed of living with me.

TANYA. What do you mean? I don't suppose she was dreaming of it happening like this.

VIKTOR. I know.

TANYA. Oh, Vitya . . . Well, have a talk with Zherekhov. Only bear in mind he's a terrible windbag and a frightful liar. Do you need money?

VIKTOR. Money? No.

TANYA. Vitya, let me give you some. I know what it's like when someone's ill. My aunt was ill for eight months. I've got two hundred rubles I put by for a summer coat, but the summer's over, look, and I haven't bought anything. So I can quite happily let you have it until the spring.

VIKTOR. No, I don't need money. I've got some. (*To the audience.*) Funny sort of day, it really was. Just one thing after another . . . one thing after another . . .

TANYA. We'll look in at my place after work, and I'll give it to you. All right?

VIKTOR. I was lying, of course. I've no money. But I don't want to take it off you.

TANYA. Idiot!

She goes up to ZHEREKHOV.

Can I interrupt you for a minute?

ZHEREKHOV *rises. They talk quietly together.*

VIKTOR. Zherekhov was obliging and affable with everyone – naturally, because being of that unhappy age when a man becomes pensionable, the old boy was fighting to keep his place. He wanted to be on the best possible terms with everybody, one after another.

ZHEREKHOV comes forward to talk to VIKTOR. TANYA follows him and inconspicuously holds VIKTOR's little finger through ZHEREKHOV's speech.

ZHEREKHOV. I'll tell you the man you want – Nevyadomsky. Did you know him? Used to work upstairs, in Construction 7. Exactly the same thing with him. Did an exchange because his mother-in-law was on her deathbed. He could tell you all about it. Of course, he had connections of some kind in the housing department. But it was a success, you know, a remarkable success. He moved his mother-in-law in, got the flat put in his name – and within three days the old lady was dead. Can you imagine? Now there he is with an exclusive luxury flat fit for a general. Several different balconies. Any amount of kitchen space, bathroom space – all kinds of space. He's even growing tomatoes on one of the balconies!

VIKTOR. How did he do it?

They both realise the DIRECTOR is within earshot.

ZHEREKHOV. What do you mean, how did he do it?

VIKTOR. Where did he start?

ZHEREKHOV. You start at the housing exchange bureau, of course. You pay three rubles and you put an announcement in the bulletin they publish.

VIKTOR. No, but you know what I mean. If someone is seriously ill, very seriously ill, and every hour counts . . .

ZHEREKHOV. There's no other way you can start. The housing exchange bureau. There are no other paths that I know of. You go and see him, though, you go and see him – he'll tell you.

VIKTOR. How do I get in touch with him?

ZHEREKHOV. Ah. That I don't know. Anyway, good luck!

ZHEREKHOV shakes VIKTOR's hand and returns to his work.

VIKTOR (*to* TANYA). Growing tomatoes on the balcony!

Growing tomatoes on his mother-in-law's grave.

TANYA. Anyway . . . downstairs at six, and we'll go straight off.

VIKTOR. You realise I've got to go out to Pavlinovo today? Mother's staying with my sister at the dacha. She's expecting me. (*To the audience.*) I knew this was dealing a blow to certain hopes she was entertaining.

TANYA. Fine. You do whatever you've got to do.

VIKTOR. No, I mean . . .

TANYA. I know what you mean! Do you really think I don't? I shan't keep you for one second. You can take the money and off you go.

VIKTOR. Her face always registered everything immediately; now the light had gone out of it. And yet every time I looked at her I thought how she would have been the better wife for me . . .

He looks at her. She smiles, touches his hand, and goes back upstage to leave. But then she stops and watches him.

Mama, Lora, Tanya, Lena, money, exchange . . . Mama, Lora, Tanya, Lena, money, exchange . . . Tanya lived in the most awkward place possible – Nagatino – way out on the wrong side of town. I'd have to leave work early, or I'd get to Pavlinovo far too late. (*To* TANYA, *quietly.*) Go at five.

TANYA *nods, smiles and goes off.*

Everyone in the department knew what was happening in my life. They were all very understanding. Once or twice a week I'd be able to leave work early. On one occasion I even used it as a pretext for dashing to the shops – was it such a terrible thing to do? – and buying a school uniform for Natashka . . . Mama, Lora, Tanya, Lena, . . .

Enter AGENT.

AGENT. Why all this agony? Just leave it to me.

The lights on the office go down. Exit the DIRECTOR *and* ZHEREKHOV.

AGENT (*to the audience*). Comrades! Urgent exchange wanted!

Single room in communal flat, brick-built, top class. Lift.
Rubbish chute. Telephone. Five minutes from Underground.
What? You want to know *which* Underground? All right, let's
say Novoslobodskaya. *Plus* superb self-contained flat on
Profsoyuznaya. About this one I'm saying nothing, because
this is a real peach. With this one you get everything you
could ever dream of. Urgent family reasons force sacrifice.
They're asking me as a favour, so I'm putting it to you, folks.
No, I'm not giving you the address just yet awhile. What, you
want to get the address off me and wave goodbye?

Finds someone in the audience responding.

Oh. I think we're in business. What am *I* looking for? I'm
looking for two rooms, self-contained, preferably in the
vicinity of Dynamo Underground . . . See you outside . . .

Exit AGENT.

Enter VIKTOR, *followed by* TANYA.

VIKTOR. We went out on the square at five, and for once . . .

He whistles and signals.

. . . there was a taxi.

They sit down side by side in the taxi. TANYA *takes his hand.*

TANYA. Why are you cross? You mustn't be. Stop, stop. Is it
what he said about that man growing the tomatoes? We're all
very different from each other, though, aren't we. My cousin
had a little boy who died. Wild grief, of course, and at the
same time some kind of new-found passionate love for
children, especially sick children. She felt sorry for them all –
she tried to do what she could to help them. And then I know
another woman whose little boy died of leukaemia. So she
conceived a terrible hatred of everyone – she longed for
everyone to die. She's delighted when she reads about
someone's death in the paper . . .

She puts her head on VIKTOR's *shoulder.*

Do you mind? I'm not being a nuisance?

VIKTOR. No, no.

> *She tickles the palm of his hand.*

> (*To the audience.*) Her caresses always had something schoolgirlish about them.

TANYA. Horrible woman! Lends you money, then forces her attentions on you. Isn't that right? I'm sorry, Vitya . . . I can't bear it . . . (*Weeps.*)

VIKTOR. Come on, now, what's the matter?

TANYA. Nothing. I just can't bear it . . .

VIKTOR. Can't bear what?

TANYA. I feel so sorry – for you, for your mother . . . and for myself, all at the same time . . .

> *He strokes her head. She sniffs. Then she moves away from him and looks out of the window of the taxi.*

VIKTOR (*to the audience*). We left the riverbank behind and followed the tramlines by some kind of factory, past a long blind brick wall. A dark crowd of men were milling around a beer stall. I could have done with a drink myself, to cheer me up a bit.

TANYA. Here we are.

VIKTOR. A new sixteen-storey block at the edge of a field. Tanya lived up on the eleventh floor.

> *They stand up.*

TANYA. Do you want the taxi to wait?

VIKTOR (*to the audience*). Obviously I wanted the taxi to wait. How would I ever find one round there?

> *He looks at her, and gives in.*

All right – let it go. I'll find one.

TANYA. Of course you will.

> TANYA *leads the way into her flat. She takes his briefcase and coat, and carries them off.*

VIKTOR. It was poor Tovt, Tanya's husband, who built this three-roomed ark. Built it himself, because this is a co-operative. They'd only just had time to move in when everything happened.

Enter TANYA. *She has taken off her coat and shoes.* VIKTOR *kicks his shoes off.*

There were newspapers down on the floor. The unfurnished room smelt of paint. I padded over the newspapers in my stockinged feet out to the kitchen and drank water from the tap. For some reason I was sure that she *would never cease to love me.*

TANYA. 'How perfect, Lord, are all Thy works . . .'

VIKTOR. Tanya knew a lot of poetry. She liked to recite it quietly, almost in a whisper.

TANYA. 'How perfect, Lord, are all Thy works!'
The sick man thought. 'These sheets,
These walls, these people in the wards;
The dark of death; the darkened streets.'

VIKTOR. Pasternak. His poem about being in hospital and expecting to die. Her memory amazed me. I don't think I know a single poem by heart. But she could go on whispering away by the hour. She has maybe twenty exercise books left over from her student days full of verses copied out in her round clear diligent schoolgirl hand – Tsvetayeva, Pasternak, Mandelshtam, Blok.

ALIK (*off left*). Mum, I'm going round to see Andryusha. We're going to be swapping stamps.

TANYA. Wait! Why haven't you said hello to Viktor Georgievich?

Enter ALIK.

ALIK. Hello.

Exit ALIK.

TANYA. And back by eight!

The door slams, off.

Not exactly the model of a well-brought-up young man.

VIKTOR. I expect he's forgotten me. I haven't been for such a time.

TANYA. Even if it was a complete stranger – he's not supposed to say hello? He hasn't forgotten you.

VIKTOR. That summer I'd lived in a state I'd never experienced before – a state of love for myself. An amazing condition! It could have been defined as habitual bliss. Because its power lay in its constancy, in the fact that it lasted for weeks, months – even continued after everything was over. But I didn't stop to think about it. I didn't ask myself why I'd been granted this happiness; what I'd done to deserve it; why *me* – not so young any more, putting on a little weight, with an unhealthy complexion and an everlasting taste of tobacco in my mouth. It seemed to me that there was nothing puzzling about it. This was how it ought to be. All in all – or so it seemed to me – I had merely entered that normal, truly human state in which all men should – and in time would – forever dwell. Tanya was quite the opposite, though. She lived in perpetual terror, in a kind of passionate perplexity. She would whisper while she embraced me, as if it were one of her poems.

TANYA. 'Why, O Lord? Why, O why?'

VIKTOR. Nothing did she ask for. Nothing did she ask about. And nothing did I promise. No, not once was there anything I ever promised. Why make promises, when I knew for sure that in any case she *would never cease to love me?* It simply used to come into my head that she would have been the better wife for me.

TANYA *fetches the money and gives it to* VIKTOR.

TANYA. Off you go, then. I know you're pressed for time.

VIKTOR. Thanks . . . I'll stay for a moment. Bit tired. Got rather a headache.

TANYA. Are you hungry? Shall I make you something?

VIKTOR. Nothing to drink, is there?

TANYA. No . . . Hold on – I think there's a bottle of brandy left somewhere that we never finished. Do you remember? Last time you were here.

Exit TANYA.

VIKTOR. I went over to the balcony. From up here on the eleventh floor there was a fine view. Open fields. The river. A village overshadowed by the cupolas of its church . . . It occurred to me that I could move in tomorrow. Into a three-roomed flat. Morning and evening I could see the river and the village, breathe the fields.

Enter TANYA *with the brandy and something to eat – sprats, two tomatoes, bread and butter.*

TANYA. Go in by bus to Serpukhovka, then by Underground. It doesn't take all that long . . . What are we going to drink to?

VIKTOR. To things being all right for you.

TANYA. Come on, then! No. We don't need to drink to that. Things will be all right for me anyway. Let's drink to things being all right for you. Yes?

VIKTOR. Very well, then.

They sit at the table.

I take it these tomatoes aren't the ones off his mother-in-law's grave?

TANYA. Because it's difficult to imagine things will ever be all right for you, Vitya. But just supposing. In spite of everything. Here's to it.

They drink the toast. Then he eats, and she hunches up, leaning her elbows on the table and gazing into space.

VIKTOR. Don't slouch!

He pats her on the shoulder in a fatherly way.

(*To the audience.*) For one moment I felt the sharpest pity.

He gets up from the table. The lights very slowly begin to go down in TANYA's *flat.*

Then I remembered that somewhere far and near, across the whole of Moscow, on the banks of this self-same river, my mother was waiting for me, and her sufferings were the sufferings of death. Tanya's sufferings belonged to life. So why should she be pitied?

TANYA *rouses herself from her thoughts, puts the things on the table back on to their tray, and carries them off.*

I took the bus to the Underground – there was no taxi, of course – changed twice, and got out at the last station of the new line. There was a fine drizzle falling. Moscow was in the distance – a line of huge blocks white against the horizon. Out here, though, there were fields with trenches dug in them for foundations. Pipes lay on the damp clay, and there was a queue for the trolleybus at the stop on the highway. Why should Tanya be pitied? There's nothing under the sun but life and death. And everything ruled by life is happiness, while everything that pertains to death is . . .

Enter VIKTOR'S FATHER.

. . . everything that pertains to death is the annihilation of happiness. Papa! Papa! What am I to do?

VIKTOR'S FATHER. Be careful, son. Take your time.

VIKTOR. Mama used to say you were always quick at making up your mind.

VIKTOR'S FATHER. Yes, of course. That was something I could always do. And you must be quite straightforward with your mother. You must tell her everything plainly, just the way it is.

VIKTOR. Papa! But you know what might happen to her!

VIKTOR'S FATHER. What do you mean?

VIKTOR. You know . . .

VIKTOR'S FATHER. Dying? My son, that's something we all come to. I was thirty-four when it happened to me. I was a healthy man – and then suddenly this illness. It was like being struck by lightning. Your mother, thanks be to God, has outlived me by thirty years.

VIKTOR. No, Papa, I can't.

VIKTOR'S FATHER. How everything's grown out here.

VIKTOR. Papa, how can I tell Mama about it?

VIKTOR'S FATHER. Listen, my son, the hardest thing of all is to know what you should do in this world . . . Almost nobody knows . . .

VIKTOR. Did you, Papa?

VIKTOR'S FATHER. Me? Well, as you may be aware, I'm rather a witty fellow. I could have devoted myself to literature. Humorous tales – that was my real vocation. Remember the ones I used to tell you? Never went anywhere without a notebook in my pocket . . . But I went to technical college and became a railway engineer instead.

A waltz can be heard, played on an ancient gramophone. The lights begin to come up on the dacha.

Enter GRANDFATHER. *He listens to* VIKTOR'S FATHER.

You know, before the Revolution you used to come out here in a kind of little horse-bus from the edge of town. I can still remember the bell it had! And the clatter of the hooves!

Enter VIKTOR'S MOTHER.

GRANDFATHER (*to* VIKTOR'S MOTHER). Dances, balls . . . If it wasn't one sort of nonsense it was another . . . I always said you were marrying someone who didn't take life seriously enough.

VIKTOR'S MOTHER. Father, he was a good, kind man. And how he loved me!

GRANDFATHER. Loved you! There's more to life than that.

VIKTOR'S MOTHER. Yes.

The music stops.

GRANDFATHER. As a conversationalist he was completely hopeless. I never knew what to talk to him about.

VIKTOR'S MOTHER. When he died in 1935 . . . you weren't

there, nor was Mama . . . and I was left alone with the children . . . it was such a moment of despair . . .

GRANDFATHER (*gently*). I know, my little girl.

VIKTOR'S MOTHER. If it hadn't been for this dacha he'd built . . . We let it to some people for the summer . . . And what about his aunts down in the Ukraine? They were starving, and he helped them. His brothers never lifted a finger.

GRANDFATHER. Yes, his brothers were nothing but clowns.

VIKTOR'S FATHER (*to* VIKTOR). My brothers fought in the Civil War. I didn't. But then nor did your grandfather, for all he was at St Petersburg University, for all his political clubs and his having to flee the country and his knowing the Grandmother of the Russian Revolution . . .

GRANDFATHER. I knew Vera Zasulich! When she was working with Plekhanov!

VIKTOR'S FATHER (*to* VIKTOR). Another Menshevik. All the revolutionaries he knew turned out to be on the losing side.

GRANDFATHER (*waves his hand dismissively*). Much it means to you.

VIKTOR'S FATHER. I never got upset at your grandfather. God preserve him! I had great respect for him . . . Do you remember, though? The story I told you about the ball up the tree?

VIKTOR *suddenly starts to laugh and nod. His* MOTHER *and* GRANDFATHER *listen, the latter slowly beginning to smile in spite of himself.*

I just made that up for fun, you know . . . As I remember, we were going to the vegetable patch, you and I, to water the cucumbers . . .

VIKTOR. And we saw Marya Petrovna trying to get a ball down from the pine-tree . . .

VIKTOR'S FATHER. Her grandson had thrown it up there. And I made up a story about how she threw one of her slippers at

it, and the slipper got stuck. So then she threw the other
slipper . . .

VIKTOR (*laughs*). Then her dress!

VIKTOR'S FATHER. And it all got stuck up the tree . . . while
Marya Petrovna sat at the bottom without a stitch on . . .

VIKTOR *is unable to speak for laughing*.

VIKTOR'S FATHER. Then Sergei the yardman tried to help her
get the things down . . .

VIKTOR (*suddenly serious*). Papa, I haven't seen your notebooks
for some time now . . . They always used to be at the bottom
of my desk . . .

VIKTOR'S FATHER. Sergei threw one boot, he threw the other
. . . his trousers, his shirt . . . And so on, until he was down
to nothing as well. Not a stitch between them . . : I got that
story published, incidentally, in a magazine called *Cranks*. Do
you remember? They paid me for it, too – twenty-four rubles
. . . Quite good money, I might tell you . . . How everything
has grown! Extraordinary! You know, I planted those birch
trees forty years ago. While they were building the house. The
Red Partisan Dacha Co-operative, it was called then. I suppose
now it comes under some local housing office, does it? With a
number instead of a name?

VIKTOR. Yes, it's Moscow now! It's on the trolleybus.

VIKTOR'S FATHER. No! Really? Moscow? On the trolleybus?
Though to tell the truth I can't quite imagine what kind of
thing a trolleybus is . . .

The waltz music is heard again. VIKTOR'S FATHER *and*
MOTHER *dance. They go off, followed by* GRANDFATHER,
and VIKTOR *himself, as the lights go down on the dacha.*

Enter AGENT.

AGENT. Exchange wanted – urgent! Urgent exchange! I'm
swapping Novoslobodskaya Underground for Tsvetnoy
Boulevard . . . then Tsvetnoy for Vernadsky Prospect . . .
Vernadsky goes to Kachalov Street, and Kachalov goes out to

Khimki-Khovrino . . . Magnificent flat, that, incidentally! You're almost in the country out there! Never mind the distance – think of the wonderful air! It's a six-way exchange, but so what? Everyone gets something out of it . . . You're getting two-and-a-half extra square metres, so what's your problem? And *you're* going to have a balcony. Though of course you've got a balcony already . . . Now, Khimki-Khovrino are going to their cousin's, and their cousin's going straight to Begovaya Street . . . The whole secret of the thing is speed . . . We're just missing one link – Begovaya doesn't want the old lady's flat! View out of the window doesn't suit her. Looks over the rubbish bins. So it looks over the rubbish bins! Put a lace curtain up! No, she's got her fads and fancies . . . and she's right . . . Everyone wants to be happy with their home. We'll just have to skip Begovaya! Leave it all to me! Give me ten minutes – I'll have the whole thing sorted out . . .

AGENT *hurries off, as the house lights go up for the interval.*

ACT TWO

The same.

Enter VIKTOR.

VIKTOR. That first year we were married Lena and I had to live out at Pavlinovo.

The lights begin to come up on the dacha.

The dacha had long since fallen into disrepair. The roof leaked.

Enter VIKTOR'S MOTHER *and* LORA *up right. They are carrying bowls to catch the leaks, laughing about it with the people who follow them on –* LENA *and her parents.* LENA'S MOTHER *is holding some kind of protection over her head.*

The porch was rotted through.

There is a splintering sound, and LENA'S MOTHER *goes through the floor. They all help her out. Then they turn to look hopefully up at the sky.*

The biggest worry was the cesspit. It kept overflowing, particularly after rain.

They all smell the smell.

An intolerable emanation would spread through the neighbourhood, mingling with the scent of lilac and phlox and lime.

A trap opens at their feet, and KALUGIN *emerges. He is very drunk.*

KALUGIN. All right. Fix it for you. Cost you . . .

> *Shows the price on his fingers. He is so drunk that he can speak more reliably with his fingers than with his tongue.*

VIKTOR'S MOTHER (*amazed*). How much?

> KALUGIN *shows her again.*

LENA. But that's bare-faced robbery!

LORA (*scornfully*). You mean you haven't come across Kalugin before? It's a den of thieves, this place.

VIKTOR. I can't smell anything.

LENA'S MOTHER. No, there's a smell all right.

VIKTOR. I don't think so.

LENA. Vitya, my poor lamb, you've got used to it.

VIKTOR. But I tell you there isn't any smell!

> KALUGIN *climbs out of the pit.*

KALUGIN. Cost you eight . . . cost eight . . . cost . . .

> *Holds his hands high up in the air to show the price, and demonstrates with gestures how all smells will be completely done away with.*

Home and dry.

> *Exit* KALUGIN.

VIKTOR'S MOTHER. I think we shall have to agree. In the first place we shall hurt his feelings if we refuse. Kalugin always repairs our cesspit, every summer . . .

LENA'S FATHER. And every summer you get done, good and proper! This Kalugin fellow of yours – he's a crook! (*To* MOTHER.) It's not right, you know, it really isn't!

VIKTOR (*still sniffing the air*). There's no smell.

VIKTOR'S MOTHER (*to* LENA'S FATHER, *mildly*). Yes, but you see, you have a different – what shall I say? – a different approach to people from us. I've known Kalugin for thirty years. He may be a crook – I'm not disputing it. But I know his family, I know his wife – sweet woman – works at the boat station here – they've got three children . . .

LENA'S FATHER. But he ought to be chucked out on his ear!

VIKTOR'S MOTHER. I don't know. I'm not sure you're right. He's not a bad man at heart.

LENA'S MOTHER. When it comes to business, my dear – you trust my husband.

LENA'S FATHER. You want a new cesspit? Leave it to me. Cement, bricks, labour – I'll fix the lot. Run out about four hundred rubles. All right? Do it in a week. And none of your enamations afterwards, I'll give you a guarantee on that.

LENA'S MOTHER. Emanations. Not enamations.

LORA. Really? How wonderful! (*Laughs.*) What wonderful relations we've acquired, Mama!

LENA'S MOTHER. Oh, we quite think the same!

LENA'S FATHER. And in a week the cesspit was finished.

He closes the trap.

LENA'S MOTHER. There you are, you see!

Enter KALUGIN.

KALUGIN. Vasilich!

KALUGIN *holds out a bottle and offers* LENA'S FATHER *a swig.*

LENA'S MOTHER. Oh look, his new-found friend!

LENA'S FATHER, *laughing and declining the drink, shakes* KALUGIN's *hand. They go off, followed by* LENA *and* HER MOTHER.

VIKTOR (*triumphantly*). How about that, then? Are you pleased with your new relations? I think he's a wonderful character. And old Kalugin hasn't taken offence. Thick as thieves together.

LORA. He sensed a kindred spirit.

VIKTOR. What do you mean?

LORA. I mean where did he hire the men? Where did he get hold of the bricks and the cement? It's a fiddle, obviously! Well, fine, good for him, I'm not going to get worked up about it . . .

VIKTOR (*flaring up*). Damn it all – you're pleased you've got a new cesspit, aren't you? And no more of those smells?

VIKTOR'S MOTHER. I'm very pleased.

LORA. How can I explain it to you . . . ? There are always smells around. If it's not one sort of smell then it's another. I can smell some kind of nasty smell, for instance. One that wasn't there before.

She moves away.

VIKTOR (*to his* MOTHER, *in irritation*). Did you see? She always gets a dig in.

VIKTOR'S MOTHER. Leave her alone. She's having such a difficult time at work.

LORA *hears this and stops.*

LORA. What's my work got to do with it?

VIKTOR. It's got to do with you somehow controlling yourself, that's what. You don't like them – all right, fine, you don't like them. There's no need to go making a performance of it all the time.

LORA (*suddenly flaring up as well*). I don't understand what sort of person would treat our mother like that, without a grain of respect!

VIKTOR. What's this? Where does this one come from?

VIKTOR'S MOTHER. Children! Stop it!

LORA. Mother's always helping others, always putting herself out for someone. And these people think of no one but themselves. How can you be so enraptured? What's happening to you, Vitya?

VIKTOR. I'm not enraptured. I'm simply asking you to be a little bit fairer . . .

LORA (*to* MOTHER). We've got to be fair . . . My God, what raving nonsense! What a brother! What a Brutus! (*Laughs.*) My dear, you've simply been *Lukyanovised*!

Exit LORA.

VIKTOR'S MOTHER. Lora . . . !

Exit VIKTOR'S MOTHER, *after her.*

VIKTOR (*to the audience*). Lukyanovised. That's from my in-laws' surname, Lukyanov. It was so difficult with Lora. She didn't understand – she just didn't understand! Her thoughts wouldn't lie smooth. They perpetually bristled and prickled, like the horsechair coming through from the lining of a badly-made suit. But how could Lora fail to understand that people aren't not loved for their vices any more than they're loved for their virtues? Your mother's your mother! Whereas my parents-in-law . . .

Enter LENA's parents. LENA'S MOTHER *watches anxiously while* LENA's FATHER *picks up the phone and waits.*

. . . Well, why get upset about them? They were simply an appurtenance of Lena's. Like her hair or her teeth or her skin.

LENA'S FATHER. Yes.

LENA'S MOTHER. Yes.

VIKTOR. My father-in-law was in truth a man to be reckoned with. Communications were his long suit. He's soon got a telephone installed at the dacha.

VIKTOR's *phone rings. He makes a face, and picks it up.*

VIKTOR. Hello?

LENA'S FATHER *hands the receiver to her* MOTHER.

LENA'S MOTHER. Hello? Can I speak to Lena, please?

VIKTOR. Lena's out, I'm afraid.

LENA'S MOTHER *puts the receiver down.*

LENA'S MOTHER (*to her husband*). Ivan!

> *She picks up the receiver again.* VIKTOR *puts his receiver down, and grins.*

> He says she's out.

VIKTOR. They loved to check everything and double-check it.

> *His phone rings. He picks it up.*

> Hello?

LENA'S MOTHER *gives her receiver to her husband.*

LENA'S FATHER. Hello? Yelena Ivanovna, please.

VIKTOR. She's out.

LENA'S MOTHER. Oh, well. Perhaps she is.

> LENA'S FATHER *and* VIKTOR *both put their receivers down.*

VIKTOR. This was their great quality in life: not to be caught napping.

> *Exit* LENA'S MOTHER.

LENA'S FATHER. Viktor, have you put the catch on the door?

VIKTOR. I have.

> LENA'S FATHER *starts to go and check.*

> For heaven's sake! Why do you bother to ask?

LENA'S FATHER. Don't take it amiss, my dear boy. I did it without thinking. I wasn't getting at you.

> *Enter* LENA'S MOTHER. *She is holding a glass of water in one hand and a pill on the palm of the other.*

LENA'S MOTHER. Ivan, what's this pill you've given me?

LENA'S FATHER. I've given you what you asked for.

LENA'S MOTHER. But what is it, then? Tell me the name.

LENA'S FATHER. You asked for Dibasol, didn't you?

LENA'S MOTHER. You've given me Dibasol?

LENA'S FATHER. Yes. Dibasol.

LENA'S MOTHER. You're sure?

LENA'S FATHER. Why are you querying it?

LENA'S MOTHER. You show me the wrapper you got it out of, please. I somehow can't help thinking this isn't Dibasol.

LENA'S FATHER fetches it.

LENA'S FATHER. Dibasol.

LENA'S MOTHER (*reads*). 'Di-ba-sol.' Yes, well, maybe it's Dibasol.

Exit LENA'S MOTHER, followed by LENA'S FATHER.

VIKTOR. It was madness, of course, to invite Grandfather to the dacha while these people were living there. My parents-in-law were a different breed. They belonged to the ranks of those who know how to get by in life.

Enter GRANDFATHER.

VIKTOR. But it couldn't be avoided. He'd only just come back to Moscow after many years in remote parts.

LENA'S MOTHER. As people say.

VIKTOR. He'd been very ill, and he needed rest. He slept on a camp bed in the passage.

GRANDFATHER (*in amazement*). Some sort of workman came today to shift the couch, and your very splendid wife and your no less splendid mother-in-law . . .

Enter LENA'S PARENTS, followed by LENA.

LENA'S MOTHER. Hello!

She waves to GRANDFATHER, who gravely inclines his head to her. LENA'S PARENTS sit down on chairs at the dacha, with their familiar air of waiting.

GRANDFATHER (*to VIKTOR still*). . . . . They both with one accord addressed him by his first name, as if he were a child or a dog. Is that the done thing now? With the father of a

nez strolling here – what would he have said? He'd probably
have said: 'Look at the type of people we're getting in
Pavlinovo these day! A lot of intellectual riff-raff in pince-nez
and Tolstoy shirts.' Yes? Don't you think? And then before
that this must have been part of some landowner's estate. He
lost all his money and sold up. Then imagine he happened to
drop by one day, and he took a look at all the clerks' and
shopkeepers' wives, all the gentlemen in bowler hats, at your
mother-in-law's uncle rolling up in a hackney cab . . .

He bows to LENA'S MOTHER.

He'd have thought to himself: 'Faugh, common trash! The
dregs of society!' Yes? Don't you think? (*Starts to laugh.*)

LENA'S MOTHER. Dregs? Why dregs? I don't understand. What
call is there for that kind of talk?

GRANDFATHER (*to* VIKTOR). Contempt is mere stupidity.
Never feel contempt for anyone.

VIKTOR'S MOTHER (*to* GRANDFATHER). No, I don't agree
with you! If we renounce contempt then we deprive ourselves
of our ultimate weapon! By all means let the feeling be inside
us, and invisible to anyone else, but be there it must.

LENA (*smiling*). I entirely agree with Grandfather. So many people
preen themselves on their – well, goodness knows what – all
kinds of myths and fantasies. It's so ridiculous!

VIKTOR (*peaceably*). Who's preening themselves on what?

LENA. Never mind! You would ask, wouldn't you?

VIKTOR'S MOTHER. Lena, preening oneself and calm contempt
are different matters.

LENA. That depends on whose point of view you're looking at it
from. I've always hated arrogance. There's nothing more
disgusting, to my way of thinking.

LORA. From your tone of voice, you'd think someone was trying
to prove that arrogance was a splendid thing. No one likes
arrogance.

LENA. Particularly when there are no grounds for it. Then it's just pure fantasy.

Smiling to herself, LORA *turns and leads the way off, followed by the rest of the party.* VIKTOR *detains* LENA.

VIKTOR. Why do you keep picking on my mother?

LENA. Forgive me, but your mother is something of a hypocrite.

VIKTOR (*explodes*). You're not going to have another go?

LENA. Vitya, what can I do? She starts talking . . . and I just feel . . .

VIKTOR. My mother – a hypocrite?

LENA. Well, she is!

VIKTOR. You live in her house, you enjoy her hospitality . . .

LENA. Rent-free, don't forget to say!

VIKTOR. You've just no conscience! Or no intelligence, or no something, I don't know what. How many times have I told you: lay off my mother! Well, then, lay off her! I won't have it! I won't! Because it'll make things difficult. It'll cause scenes. It'll make things difficult for you, too. Good God, even a child can learn to keep its fingers out of the fire!

Enter VIKTOR'S MOTHER.

LENA. You know what? I'm sick and tired of this! Your mother is some kind of sacred cow. I have to creep around on tiptoe.

Enter LORA.

So listen – tomorrow I'm leaving this marvellous dacha of yours! I've had enough! And please don't try to phone me!

LENA *runs off.*

VIKTOR'S MOTHER. Vitya! Why are you behaving like this?

LORA. Leave him alone, Mama! He's right!

VIKTOR. It all ended with Lena having her great heart attack in the middle of the night, and the ambulance being called, and her mother shouting about selfishness and cruelty . . .

Enter LENA, *with a blanket round her, attended by her*
MOTHER, *and followed by her* FATHER *carrying her bag.*

LENA'S MOTHER (*to* VIKTOR, *hysterical*). Yes, yes, yes!

LENA'S FATHER (*shouts*). Vera!

LENA'S MOTHER (*shouts back*). Vanya!

VIKTOR'S MOTHER (*reproachfully*). Vitya!

LORA. Mama!

LENA'S PARENTS *lead* LENA *off, with* VIKTOR'S
MOTHER *and* LORA *hurrying after them.*

VIKTOR. . . . and everyone departing, and silence descending
upon the dacha.

Enter GRANDFATHER. *He sits down peaceably.*

When just the two of us were left, Grandfather and myself . . .

VIKTOR *sits in another chair at the dacha.*

Perhaps I should give her a ring, all the same. What do you
think?

GRANDFATHER. I don't know.

VIKTOR. Although of course she behaved appallingly.

GRANDFATHER. I've got out of touch with women. Can't
understand them any more.

VIKTOR. No, Lena certainly, I mean, *loves* me, I can assure you
of that . . . I mean when there are no idiots around . . . That
simply is a fact . . . She has her faults, of course, and they're
considerable ones . . . She's quarrelsome – the slightest thing
and she's up in the air about it . . .

GRANDFATHER (*looks thoughtfully at the cesspit*). They make you
dig a pit that size in two days. Out where I was. I became a
great expert on digging.

VIKTOR. Lukyanovised . . . Oh, rubbish! Who's been
Lukyanovised? What's all this about 'Lukyanovised'?

GRANDFATHER. The number of people I've buried! So many

there's nothing frightening about it now. No! Nothing frightening at all.

VIKTOR. To phone or not to phone.

GRANDFATHER. It's a shame – I'd like to know what will happen next in the world. All my long life up to now doesn't concern me at all. There's nothing more foolish than looking for ideals in the past. But the future, now, . . . yes, that does interest me.

VIKTOR. Do you remember what it was like on the other side of the river? Meadows, cows . . . Now there's a bathing-beach, deckchairs, stalls selling beer . . . And in the distance – towers, cranes, mountains of human habitation. Each year there's been some small detail changed. Now fourteen years have gone by and it turns out that everything has been Lukyanovised – conclusively and hopelessly Lukyanovised.

GRANDFATHER. By no means everything. Not everything at all.

VIKTOR. Perhaps it's not a bad thing? And if it happens to everything – to the river, to the riverbank and the grass – then perhaps it's natural, perhaps it's the way it ought to be? To phone or not to phone? (*To the audience.*) I phoned that evening. Grandfather died four years later.

A crematorium. A funeral march is heard over loudspeakers. GRANDFATHER *and* VIKTOR *go off, and the congregation enters:* VIKTOR'S MOTHER, LORA, FELIX, LENA, NATASHKA, LENA'S PARENTS, AUNT ZHENYA, *and* COUSIN MARINA. VIKTOR *enters hurriedly and joins them, loading tins into this briefcase. The others look around at him.*

VIKTOR (*embarrassed*). I came straight from work. I happened to pass a shop where they'd got some tins of salmon. Lena loves tinned salmon . . .

He finds some discreet hiding-place for the briefcase.

The funeral march ends, and from the loudspeakers comes an oration. The speaker is an elderly woman. We hear only odd snatches between the rest of the dialogue.

ELDERLY WOMAN (*over loudspeaker*). Today, as we take our leave of an unforgettable man, I cannot help recalling the year 1911, when our fortunes were at their lowest ebb . . .

VIKTOR (*to his* MOTHER). Who's this?

VIKTOR'S MOTHER. She was a famous terrorist. One of the Maximalists. She threw a bomb at someone.

ELDERLY WOMAN (*over loudspeaker*). . . . We were living through difficult times . . . I recall a meeting with Paul Lafargue . . . And Laura Marx . . .

Enter LYOVKA BUBRIK. VIKTOR *glances at him superciliously.*

VIKTOR (*to* BUBRIK). Hello. (*To* LORA.) Lyovka Bubrik. What's he doing here?

LORA. Well, he's a relative of some kind.

ELDERLY WOMAN (*over loudspeaker*). Our headquarters were in a little working-class district on the outskirts of Paris . . .

LENA *weeps, and noisily blows her nose.*

VIKTOR (*to himself*). Mustn't forget the briefcase, mustn't forget the briefcase . . . How old Mother's face is, and how like a child's, all at the same time . . .

ELDERLY WOMAN (*over loudspeaker*). I remember a conversation I had with him. He was talking about presence of mind, about the courage that life demands . . .

LENA (*through her tears*). He was such a good, kind man. I loved him. I loved him more than anyone . . .

The lights on the crematorium go down and music plays the congregation out.

LORA (*to* VIKTOR). Are you coming on to Aunt Zhenya's?

AUNT HENYA. You will, won't you, Vitya?

VIKTOR. Of course. Why do you ask?

LORA. We wouldn't ask, if you were on your own. We're always glad to see you – you know that . . . Anyway, you please yourself . . .

VIKTOR. We'll probably come on a bit later . . .

LENA. Why? You go! I'm not feeling too good, but you go!

VIKTOR. No, we probably won't come. Lena's got a headache.

LORA. Right. I see. (*Gives him pills.*) Something for a headache. Give it to Lena. Goodbye.

Everyone has divided into two groups. VIKTOR'S MOTHER, LORA, FELIX, AUNT ZHENYA, COUSIN MARINA, *and* LYOVKA BUBRIK *go off one way,* LENA, HER PARENTS, *and* NATASHKA *the other.* VIKTOR *moves after his wife's party.*

VIKTOR. Something else had died with Grandfather, something not directly connected with him – some kind of threads binding the family together. In my sister's eyes I wasn't part of the family any more – I was something associated with Lena and her parents . . . Briefcase!

He rushes back to retrieve it.

The next body was already waiting. But what a place to meet Lyovka Bubrik! In a crematorium! He didn't want to see me. Even though he was a relative of some kind.

Enter GRANDFATHER, *as the lights comes up on the dacha.*

GRANDFATHER. What do you mean, 'of some kind'? He's the grandson of my brother Stepan, who died of the Spanish influenza in 1919. That makes him my great-nephew and your second cousin. Why, you've been friends since you were children.

He sits in the chair where he was sitting before.

VIKTOR. Yes, yes. We *were* friends. But then we fell out!

Enter LENA *in the flat, followed by her parents.* LENA *gets on with chores while her parents sit and wait.*

Enter VIKTOR'S MOTHER *and* LORA *at the dacha. Enter* BUBRIK *in another part of the set.*

LENA. I was very nice to that Lyovka of yours. I even begged my father to go and see Prusakov, and get him to do something for Lyovka.

GRANDFATHER. Yes, and what happened in the end?

VIKTOR'S MOTHER. It wasn't good enough, my son, your behaviour over Lyovka Bubrik.

BUBRIK. Oh, nonsense! I've forgotten about it, anyway. It was all so long ago.

GRANDFATHER (*to* VIKTOR). Yes, lad, your mother and I expected you to turn out rather differently. Nothing very terrible happened, of course. You're not a bad fellow. But you're not a very remarkable one, either.

VIKTOR (*heatedly*). What's it got to do with me? It all just happened! It wasn't because *I* wanted it. (*To the audience.*) Lyovka arrived in Moscow after he'd been working in the oilfields out in the Urals, and he didn't have a job. I really and truly did try to help him. Lena tried, too. She talked to her father, and her father found out from Prusakov about this job in oil and gas machinery. It was all done for Lyovka's benefit!

LENA. Of course it was. My father went to great pains to help him.

LENA'S FATHER. This Zubrik fellow of yours . . .

LENA'S MOTHER. Bubrik!

LENA'S FATHER. Anyway, there's a job for him. Prusakov went round to see Kovrigin. Kovrigin gave Malinkin a ring. Malinkin got on to Kalinkin, and his people promised they'd fix it all. Something to do with engineering. Hundred and eighty a month.

LORA. Good money. And no emanations, either.

LENA'S FATHER. Oh, he'll be as happy as a pig in muck.

LENA'S MOTHER. Vanya!

LENA (*laughs*). Wonderful, isn't it? We've landed this nice little plum for Lyovka – a hundred and eighty a month, while here *we* sit on a hundred and thirty.

VIKTOR. You mean, I could . . . ? What – not tell him about it? Just go along myself and . . . ? But I can't possibly . . .

LENA. Yes, you can. He won't know anything about it.

VIKTOR. In the first place he *will*, and in the second place . . .

VIKTOR'S MOTHER (*warningly*). Vitya!

LORA (*waves her hand dismissively*). Mama, you're wasting your breath.

LENA. So you'd like your son to stay in his present job, would you, and go on slaving away for a pittance? Three hours travelling each day? That really is hypocrisy!

LENA'S MOTHER. Yes.

LENA'S FATHER. Yes.

LENA. In your heart of hearts, of course, you're glad your son will be doing better for himself. But you have to put on a show of high-mindedness. Well, I'm more honest that you are. All due respect to Lyovka – but for some strange reason I love my husband more.

VIKTOR'S MOTHER. You're very much mistaken, Lena, if you think I can be glad at someone else's expense.

LORA. It would be nice to know how you'll explain all this to Lyovka.

LENA. Yes, it's just the outward form that interests you, isn't it. How to explain, how to present it. What I care about is the essence of the thing. About making my life – your son's life – your brother's – about making my family's life easier and happier. So!

LENA'S FATHER. I never had any blueprints laid down for me by *my* father, and I've always expected her to act likewise. She's right.

VIKTOR. It was terrible . . . I couldn't sleep at night. I wavered in an agony of indecision. But, gradually, what had been impossible even to contemplate, let alone do, turned into something tiny and insignificant, something neatly packaged like a capsule to be swallowed – that *had* to be swallowed, even, for the sake of one's health – in spite of the foulness it contained inside. In fact no one notices the foulness. And they all swallow the capsules.

BUBRIK. I forgave him. Though really, what was there to forgive? Why should he let me have the job if he needed it as badly as all that himself?

LORA (*to* BUBRIK). Your wife didn't forgive him, though, and she never will. (*To the* OTHERS.) Lyovka couldn't get a job anywhere. They were living on what they could borrow. While *he* was already sitting at Lyovka's job!

BUBRIK. Well, good luck to them, the pair of them.

VIKTOR. It was all dead and buried. It had almost vanished from people's memory.

GRANDFATHER. All the same, it wasn't Lyovka who ended up in the job, was it. It was you.

VIKTOR. But I'm saying it just happened to turn out like that. Do you think it was easy for me? I almost died! I began to have these violent headaches!

LENA. He was in agony. And it wasn't him who wanted to do it. It was me who persuaded him.

VIKTOR'S MOTHER (*smiling*). I see, Lena.

LENA. Because it was the reasonable thing to do! With people like you and your family there's only one way to fight – by behaving *reasonably*.

LENA'S MOTHER. Yes.

LENA'S FATHER. There's no other way.

LENA. You remember how it was getting *my* job?

VIKTOR. She knew how to sink her teeth into what she wanted . . .

LORA. Like a bulldog. Such a nice-looking woman – a bulldog with a neat hair-style and a complexion that was always agreeably tanned. No, I give Lena her full due. For a lot of things.

VIKTOR. And she didn't let go until whatever it was she'd got her teeth into came away. A great characteristic to have! A decisive one in life! A real man's characteristic! Later I was offered a job in Turkmenia. Out beyond the Caspian, in the Kara Kum Desert – not all that far from where Lora was working part of each year on her archaeological expeditions with Felix. It was an enticing idea. I sometimes used to wake up in the morning and think: 'Wouldn't it be nice . . .' And everything looked as sharp and transparent as if I'd climbed a mountain on a clear day and I was looking at the world far below.

LENA. Vitya, why are you fooling yourself? You can't go anywhere away from us. I don't know if you love us, but you can't leave us, you can't! That's all over! You're too late!

LENA'S MOTHER. Yes.

LENA'S FATHER. Yes.

LENA. Yes.

VIKTOR. My own thoughts exactly – and ones that frightened me. 'No trips or expeditions! Not for more than a week!' – that was her wish.

LORA. A poor simple-hearted wish, with iron teeth-marks in it.

GRANDFATHER. Yes, lad, your mother and I really had hopes of you.

Exit GRANDFATHER.

VIKTOR. It was all dead and buried. It had almost vanished from people's memory.

Everyone except VIKTOR *goes off.*

It stirred again, though, three or four years later. This was, what, five years ago – almost the last time Lena ever went to my mother's. It was at my mother's flat, on a winter's day – her birthday, at the end of February.

VIKTOR'S MOTHER *flat in town. Snow on the roofs outside. Enter* VIKTOR'S MOTHER, *followed by* AUNT ZHENYA, COUSIN MARINA, LORA, *and* FELIX. *They are all in a*

*cheerful bustling mood. They are carrying a table-cloth and dishes,
with which they lay the table.*

Mama was still perfectly well then.

VIKTOR'S MOTHER. Wonderfully well!

VIKTOR. Not a hint of any trouble! She used to go skiing at
     Pavlinovo!

VIKTOR'S MOTHER. Yes, yes, I did!

Enter LENA *and* NATASHKA. LENA *irritably pulls*
NATASHKA's *stockings straight and brushes imaginary dust off
her coat.*

VIKTOR. Lena never liked going to her mother-in-law's.

LENA. I only go through ordeals like this to please you.

VIKTOR. As she always did. What could I do? She didn't like it –
     she couldn't make herself like it – she found it unbearable.
     Everything about it irritated her. However delicious the food,
     however polite the conversation, it was no use. It was like
     heating the street.

VIKTOR'S MOTHER. Yes.

LENA. Yes.

LORA. Yes.

     VIKTOR's *party go into his* MOTHER's *flat. Polite greetings are
     exchanged all round.*

VIKTOR (*to* NATASHKA). So are you pleased to see Granny,
     then, poppet?

NATASHKA. Mm.

VIKTOR. You like coming to Granny's?

NATASHKA. Yes, I do.

LENA (*smiling*). I like coming to Granny's, say, but I've got to go
     to bed nice and early. Papa mustn't sit around forever, say, so
     he has to be dragged away from the table by force. At half-
     past nine, say, we get up and go.

Everyone sits down at the table.

VIKTOR. And everything would have gone off all right . . . if it hadn't been for my cousin Marina. Whenever she and Lena met at family gatherings they'd start clawing each other's eyes out.

COUSIN MARINA. Oh, Natashka! What a big girl you've grown!

LENA. You don't change at all, though, Marina! Absolutely not at all! Still perfectly preserved!

COUSIN MARINA. Thank you! That's a very sweet . . . verb. You're in very good shape yourself!

LENA. Me? (*Laughs.*) I'm a frightful sight!

AUNT ZHENYA. Someone's fishing for compliments.

LENA (*to* AUNT ZHENYA). No, but your nephew treats me so badly! Always on at me about something!

AUNT ZHENYA. I can just imagine. Have some fish!

LENA. I won't, thank you. (*TO* MARINA.) So, Marina, how are things with you? The same as ever?

COUSIN MARINA. Of course! And you? Are you still working at the same place?

LENA. Certainly. You're still where you were, are you? Some kind of – forgive me – publishing-house, isn't it?

VIKTOR. Their conversations always reminded me of a water-polo match, where the players kick each other under the surface, out of sight from the spectators. But *I* could see. I knew what was going on.

LENA. Have you published anything interesting recently, then?

COUSIN MARINA. We've published a few things. What kind of material is that? Where did you manage to find it?

VIKTOR. What the conversation was in fact about was this:

LENA. So what, then, Marina – you still haven't had so much as a nibble from anyone? I'm sure you haven't, and never will, either, because you're on the shelf, my dear.

COUSIN MARINA. Well, that doesn't worry me, because I'm living a creative life. Unlike you. You work, you see, and I create. I live by creating.

LENA. What's all this creating you're babbling about? Have you personally edited or published so much as one good book?

COUSIN MARINA. Of course. But there's no point in talking to you about it because it couldn't be of any possible interest to you. All you're interested in is consumer goods. You're a philistine.

VIKTOR. Marina couldn't abide philistinism. Oh dear, philistines! When she started to seethe about people who didn't accept Picasso, smoke and flames would come out of her mouth.

LENA (*aside to* VIKTOR). If your cousin doesn't stop needling me I'm going to get up and go.

VIKTOR. Why, what did she say to you?

LENA. And you can stay here!

VIKTOR. What's all this about?

LENA. You could hear perfectly well!

COUSIN MARINA. Won't you have some of this? Please . . .

LENA (*handing the dish back*). Please . . .

AUNT ZHENYA. Do have some!

LENA. No! No, thank you.

LORA. Are you on a diet?

AUNT ZHENYA. Just this little piece, look.

FELIX. The crab salad is excellent.

LORA. Where did you get the shrimps?

FELIX. This potato salad is very nice.

VIKTOR'S MOTHER. Have some more.

LORA (*to* LENA). Tomatoes.

LENA. Well, in my opinion that's all hypocrisy.

LORA. Hypocrisy?

AUNT ZHENYA. In what way hypocrisy?

LENA. Yes, yes – hypocrisy!

COUSIN MARINA. Liking Picasso is hypocrisy?

LENA. Of course it is, because people who say they like Picasso usually can't make head nor tail of it – and that's plain hypocrisy!

COUSIN MARINA. My God? Hold me up, someone! (*Laughs.*) Liking Picasso is hypocrisy! Oh dear, oh dear!

LENA (*shouting*). What are you trying to prove to me?

General uproar. LENA *and* COUSIN MARINA *jump up from their chairs.* LORA *looks at them contemptuously.* LENA *and* COUSIN MARINA *are shouting each other down.*

COUSIN MARINA. If there was *something* you understood! How about Van Gogh? Or Salvador Dali? Pure philistinism!

LENA. Abstract whatever it is! Paul Jackson! Pure hypocrisy!

COUSIN MARINA. Paul Jackson? Who's this Paul Jackson?

LENA. I don't care who Paul Jackson is! Because it's all hypocrisy!

COUSIN MARINA. My God! And will you explain, please, what you mean by hypocrisy?

LENA. I mean everything that's not done naturally, everything that's done with some kind of ulterior motive, with the intention of showing yourself in a better light.

COUSIN MARINA (*beginning to laugh*). Aha! So in other words you're behaving with hypocrisy when you come to see your mother-in-law on her birthday and bring her a box of chocolates?

VIKTOR'S MOTHER (*reproachfully*). Now, Marina, why must you say a thing like that?

LENA (*to* VIKTOR) I predicted all this. Eat up, please. (*To the others.*) My relations with my mother-in-law are not as good as they might be, it's true. I came to wish her a happy birthday, though, not out of hypocrisy, but because Vitya asked me to.

AUNT ZHENYA. Well, why don't we talk about something else? What news of Lyovka Bubrik?

The others all freeze.

VIKTOR'S MOTHER. I'll tell you afterwards.

LORA. It's a delicate subject.

AUNT ZHENYA. Delicate? Is he? What's wrong with him?

COUSIN MARINA. Mama! Lyovka Bubrik!

AUNT ZHENYA. Vitya, for a long time I simply could not believe that you had behaved like that . . . It's not at all the sort of thing I associate with you.

VIKTOR'S MOTHER. Zhenya!

LENA. But you would with me? With me, perhaps, you would associate it?

AUNT ZHENYA. You, Lena, I of course know less well . . .

LENA. Oh, so you think I'm the one who was responsible for everything? And your Viktor here had nothing to do with it?

VIKTOR'S MOTHER. I'm not excusing Vitya.

LENA. But all the same, it was me, was it?

LORA. Vitya! I beg you!

LENA. Yes, of course, I'm capable of anything! Your Viktor's a good little boy. I've corrupted him.

VIKTOR'S MOTHER. But you explained it to Lyovka that way yourself. I remember very clearly.

LENA. Never mind how I explained it! I was looking after my husband! I was protecting his good name! And you have no right, you have simply no right . . .

NATASHKA (*frightened*). Mama!

VIKTOR. Stop shouting!

LENA. Well, you traitor! I don't want to exchange another word with you!

She seizes NATASHKA *by the hand and drags her away from the table.*

Why do you always keep quiet while I'm being insulted?

Exit LENA *and* NATASHKA. VIKTOR *runs after them, then gives up the chase. The remaining guests at the table sit silenced and still. The lights on* VIKTOR'S MOTHER's *flat begin to fade.*

VIKTOR (*to the audience*). After that – ruin . . . I ran downstairs, and slithered on the frozen puddles. Lena and Natashka, in their ridiculous flight, were jumping aboard a trolleybus. The doors closed, and I didn't know where to go next, or what would happen.

He sits in the armchair in his own flat, dejected.

I couldn't go anywhere. The house was coming down about my ears, and I'd nowhere to go and no one to turn to.

The guests around the table quietly depart, taking the dishes and the tablecloth with them. VIKTOR *is alone. He recovers himself.*

That was five years ago. Now here I was, on my way from Tanya's to the dacha, getting off the trolley-bus in Pavlinovo. And the only thing I could think about was how to ask my mother for the key, after everything that had happened, how to tell her about all this business of the exchange.

The dacha. Night. Darkness at the window. Enter LORA *and* FELIX, *carrying a bucket of paste, old newspapers, and scissors. They begin to cut the newspaper into strips, and paste them over the gaps in the window-frame right to make it draughtproof.*

VIKTOR. I stood in front of the old dacha in Pavlinovo and looked in through the window. The lights were on, and I could see Lora. It was growing dark in the garden, and I viewed her as if she were an image on a fluorescent screen, as if she were a stranger. She and Felix were sealing up the house for winter. I saw the ageing and illness that were her reward for the years of archaeological expeditions in the desert. I saw the rough anguish of her heart, gripped now by one single concern . . .

He goes into the dacha.

(*To* LORA, *nodding at the paste and newspapers.*) Already?

LORA. It's nearly the end of October . . . Mama's asleep, but I expect she'll wake up in a minute. She had a bad turn at half-past four. The pains began again. We were very frightened – I wanted to call the ambulance – but Mama said there was no point, it would be better to get the doctor. She took some of her pills, and the pain went.

VIKTOR. So what it is? What's happening?

LORA. Mama's very depressed. Such a relapse all of a sudden. It's the first time since she came out of hospital. She says it's just like it was in May – the pain's as bad as it was then, and it's in the same place.

VIKTOR (*somehow indignant*). But I rang you some time after three! Everything was all right then.

LORA. Yes, everything was fine. But an hour later . . .

Exit FELIX.

Any moment now Felix is going to start about getting down to Turkmenia. I beg you – tell him you're definitely against it. Tell him you can't possibly look after . . .

Enter FELIX, *carrying a large packet of photographs. He shows them to* VIKTOR, *humming to himself.*

FELIX. This is Lora at the dig, with some of the pottery . . . This is her handsome husband . . Our workmen, Ashirka and Chari . . . My camel, Lyop-Lyop . . . Have to go at the end of November. Beginning of December at the latest. Be there by the fifteenth without fail.

LORA. You will be, you will be! Don't get excited! I've said you can go. Of course you've got to, if there are eighteen people waiting for you.

FELIX. Unfortunately, you've got to go, too. There are eighteen people waiting for *you*.

LORA. But we agreed – first you go out . . .

FELIX. How do you see things developing, though?

LORA. Well, how do *you* see things developing?

FELIX. There is Vitya, after all. Her own son.

LORA. That's enough about Vitya. Forget about Vitya! Anyway, now isn't the time to talk about it.

FELIX *begins to go out, then stops*.

FELIX. So when do you suggest we talk about it? I have to wire Mamedov.

LORA *dismisses him with an impatient wave of the hand. Exit* FELIX.

LORA. Felix is a good, kind man. He loves Mama; Mama loves him. But he can be very obtuse at times. I wonder now and again if it isn't slightly pathological. There are some things it's impossible to explain to him. You simply have to tell him, quite categorically; it's thus and so, look, and that's all there is to it! And in the end he accepts it. You must tell him firmly: *No*! I *can't* stay with Mama! And then he'll stop nagging. How *could* you stay with her, in actual fact? You'd take Mama to your place? You'd move in here?

VIKTOR (*shrugs*). I don't know.

LORA. I won't agree to your doing either. Of course it's important for Felix to go. It's important for me, too – but what can we do?

VIKTOR (*slowly*). We could try exchanging Mama's room and our room for a two-room flat. So that we and Mama could live together – Mama, Lena, Natashka, and me. But that's quite a business. Not all that easy to do. Although at the moment a possibility does exist.

LORA. This is Lena's idea?

VIKTOR. Why should it be Lena's idea? It's my idea. An idea I've had for a long time.

LORA. Well, just don't say anything to Felix about this idea of yours, all right? He might take you up on it. It's the last thing Mama needs. The state she's in, to have to put up with this on top of it all . . . Because I know what'll happen. For a start it'll all be sweetness and light, and then irritation will set in. No, it's an appalling idea. A real nightmare. Brr – I can just imagine it!

She wriggles her shoulders with an expression of fear and disgust.

No, thank you – I'll stay with Mama. I'm not going anywhere. Felix will manage somehow.

Enter FELIX. He gets on with the work again. Pause. LORA smiles at her thoughts.

VIKTOR. What?

LORA. Nothing . . . I often wonder, though, why you don't join a co-operative and build yourself a flat. It doesn't cost all that much. Your in-laws will help. They're so fond of their grand-daughter after all.

FELIX. What's all this about?

LORA. I'm just saying why don't Viktor and Lena build themselves a co-operative flat? A small one, with two rooms. Wouldn't that be a good idea?

VIKTOR (*choking with anger*). We don't want a flat! We don't want one – do you understand? *I* don't want one, at any rate. Not me, not me! I don't want anything! Absolutely nothing! Just to make things all right for our mother. She's always wanted to live with me, though. Not with you – with me. You know that. And if it would help her at all now . . .

LORA *sits and covers her face with her hands.*

VIKTOR (*to the audience*). Idiot! What am I saying this for? But I *don't* in fact want anything! Felix, just make yourself scarce for a moment, will you?

Exit FELIX.

VIKTOR (*to LORA*). Come on, stop that, now . . .

LORA (*still with her palms pressed against her face*). You do as you please. Just as you please. If she wants to, then go ahead . . .

VIKTOR *and* LORA *sit in silence.*

Enter AGENT.

AGENT. We're all hanging by a thread! You realise? Thirteen flats! Because if Mama here, God forbid, should happen to . . . well, it'll all be down the drain immediately. All the colossal labour, all the wear and tear on the nerves, that have gone into putting together this amazing structure. It's a real work of art. A thirteen-way exchange! I'll never get it set up again. Just look at the beauty of it! This lot are going to Tsvetnoy Boulevard, and Tsvetnoy are going to Vernadsky Prospect. From there we go to Kachalov Street, out to Khimi-Khovrino, and back to Vakhtangov Street by way of the Arbat. From Vakhtangov by way of Arts Theatre Passage into Upper Taganka Alley. Then we go to a cycling champion on Lilac Boulevard – from him to this old lady – and from the old lady we go . . . Hold on. Where do we go after the old lady? My God, the size of Moscow! I'm getting on in years. My brain's not what it was. I've buried my wife. What do I want with all this excitement? I get my pension, that's quite enough. So what – I want more than other people? No – I must finish it! I must get there! Oh, of course – the old lady's going in with this lot!

Exit AGENT.

Enter FELIX *with a piece of paper.*

FELIX. A message today, look, from Mamedov. The poor chap wants to know if he's to buy sleeping-bags for us. He's at base in Chardzhou. We have to reply at once saying whether he's to get them or not. Wire him, even.

LORA (*listens*). Mama!

LORA *and* VIKTOR *jump to their feet. Enter their* MOTHER, *in her dressing-gown. She is holding a hot water bottle.*

VIKTOR'S MOTHER. Well, you see what a fine state of affairs we've got here!

She walks carefully to the sofa, and sits down. FELIX *fetches a down bed-cover from off.* VIKTOR *and* LORA *tuck her up in it and make her comfortable with cushions.*

VIKTOR (*with passionate reproach*). But I was talking to you on the phone only this morning!

LORA. How is it now? Here's your medicine. And put the thermometer under.

Exit FELIX.

VIKTOR'S MOTHER. Now it feels just as if . . .

She leans forward slightly.

Just as if it's all right. More or less nothing at all. Goodness me, what a nonsense it all is! It's a mean trick to play on anyone, though, a stomach ulcer. I feel most indignant. I'd like to register a protest. Send for the complaints book. Only who to complain to? God, do you think?

LORA. Are you comfortable? Come this way a bit . . . Take the thermometer, and I'll bring you some tea in a moment. Give me your hot water bottle.

Exit LORA. VIKTOR *sits down. His* MOTHER *puts the thermometer under her arm.*

VIKTOR'S MOTHER. Oh yes – Vitya! It's a good thing you've come. I had a great argument with Lora today, and we've got a bar of chocolate on the outcome. You see that picture you did when you were a child? Over there, on the windowsill? Lora found it in the green cupboard. She says you did it in the summer of 1939 or 1940, but I think it was after the war. When who was it was living here – do you remember? What was he called? Such a nasty man. He had some kind of Eastern name. I've forgotten, you'll have to tell me.

VIKTOR. I don't remember.

He looks gloomily at the picture, displeased by it.

I did this before the war, though. The ornamental fence wasn't there afterwards. They burnt it.

VIKTOR'S MOTHER. What's happening about this job you're going on?

VIKTOR. I'm not going.

VIKTOR'S MOTHER. I hope not on account of my being ill?

VIKTOR. No, it's been postponed, that's all. What's your being ill got to do with it?

VIKTOR'S MOTHER. Vitya, I don't want any of you to have your work interfered with in the slightest. Because work comes first. All old ladies fall ill – that's our trade. We lie in bed and groan for a bit, then we get up on our feet again – while you lose precious time and mar your work. It's not right. (*Lowers her voice.*) I'm being plagued by Lora now, for example. She tells me the most unconscionable lies. She says she's not obliged to go away this year. Felix, too – he mumbles to himself and evades the question. But I know what they're up to! Why do they do it? Am I really a helpless old lady who can't be left on her own? Not at all! I may have relapses, of course, like today. Even a lot of pain – I admit that – because it's a slow process. But essentially I'm getting better. And I shall do it perfectly well on my own. You're close by – I've got a phone. Great heavens above, what's all the fuss?

Enter LORA *with the hot water bottle.*

LORA. Fuss? What fuss? Mama, don't get excited. Let Vitya do the talking – you just listen. What were you getting so excited about?

VIKTOR'S MOTHER. Certain people make me cross when they don't tell me the truth.

LORA. Oh, I see. Come on, now. Give me the thermometer . . . Normal. Vitya, don't let Mother get excited, do you hear? Otherwise I'll chase you out. And come and have supper in ten minutes.

Exit LORA. *Enter* LENA *in the flat. She picks up the phone.*

VIKTOR'S MOTHER (*whispers*). How can we arrange it so that old people could be ill in peace, and not spoil things for their children . . . ?

LORA (*off*). Vitya! Phone!

> VIKTOR *picks up the receiver.*

VIKTOR. Hello?

LENA. It's me. How are things at that end? How's your mother?

VIKTOR. All right. About the same.

LENA. You'll be staying the night, will you?

VIKTOR. Probably. By the time we've eaten . . .

LENA. Give her lots of love from me. Lots of love from Natashka, too.

> VIKTOR *inclines his head to his* MOTHER, *as if he is passing on the greeting.*

And don't forget the key.

VIKTOR. What?

LENA. The key. To your mother's flat.

VIKTOR. Good night.

> *He puts down the receiver.* LENA *puts down her receiver, too, and goes off. The lights on the flat go down.*

VIKTOR (*to the audience*). It was up to me, and me alone. I was the only one who could decide whether to ask for the key or not. And an hour or two later, just before I went to bed, I seized my opportunity. I went into Mama's room, and . . . I said it. (*To* MOTHER.) Mama, there's also this possibility: we could do an exchange, and all move into one flat together. Then Lora wouldn't be tied down.

VIKTOR'S MOTHER. Exchange with you?

VIKTOR. Not with me – with someone else. Get a larger flat, so that you and I could live in the same place.

VIKTOR'S MOTHER. Oh, like that. Of course. I understand. I used to long to live with you and Natashka. Not now, though.

VIKTOR. Why not?

VIKTOR'S MOTHER. I don't know. I've had no desire to for a
long time now.

Pause. VIKTOR *is stunned*.

You've done your exchange already, Vitya. It's over and
finished with. A long, long while ago. It happens all the time.
Every day. So don't be surprised, Vitya. And don't be angry.
That's what happens. Just like that. Imperceptibly . . .

She closes her eyes. She wants to sleep. VIKTOR *tiptoes away*.

VIKTOR (*to the audience*). I slept in the room on the verandah
where I'd lived with Lena, that first summer.

The lights dim, leaving only VIKTOR *and his* MOTHER
illuminated.

The rug that Lena had put up on the wall was still there. But
the beautiful green wallpaper with the raised pattern had faded
noticeably, and grown bald. As I was going to sleep I thought
about my old water-colour: the bit of garden, the fence, the
porch – and on the porch, our dog Nelda. She looked so much
like a sheep. How could Lora have forgotten that we didn't
have Nelda after the war? After the war, though, I drew and
painted like a madman. I couldn't be separated from my
album . . . If only I hadn't failed my exams and thrown myself
into the first job that came along out of sheer misery . . . Then
I started to think about the trip I should have been making
out to Golyshmanovo. I saw the room in the barrack hut
where I'd spent six weeks the previous year . . . And I
thought about how Tanya would have been the better wife for
me . . .

LENA *enters the flat, and stands waiting*.

VIKTOR. Two days later Mama phoned me at work and said
she'd agree to the move. All she asked was that we did it
quickly.

LENA's *parents enter and help* VIKTOR *to start carrying things
out of the flat*.

VIKTOR'S MOTHER *watches them from the divan as they work.* LORA, FELIX, NATASHKA, VIKTOR'S FATHER *and* GRANDFATHER *and* TANYA *enter quietly. They gather around* VIKTOR'S MOTHER, *and watch with her.*

The lights go down.

THE PRONUNCIATION OF THE NAMES

The following is an approximate practical guide. In general, all stressed a's are pronounced as in 'far' (the sound is indicated below by 'aa') and all stressed o's as in 'more' (they are written below as 'aw'). All unstressed a's and o's are thrown away and slurred. The u's are pronounced as in 'crude'; they are shown below as 'oo'. A y at the beginning of a syllable, in front of another vowel, is pronounced as a consonant (i.e. as in 'yellow', not as in 'sky').

The Characters:

*Veek*tor (*Veek*tor Ge-*or*-gi-yev-ich *Dmit*ri-yev – *Veet*ya)
*Lyay*na (Yel-*yay*-na Ee*vaa*novna)
Nat*aash*ka
Look*yaa*nov, Ee*vaan* – *Vaan*ya
*Vye*ra
*Law*ra – *Law*rochka
*Fye*lix
*Zhen*ya
Ma*ree*na
*Lyov*ka *Boob*rik
*Zhe*rekhov
*Sneet*kin
*Taan*ya
Ka*loo*gin

Other names occurring in the play, in alphabetical order:

Andryusha – And-*ryoosh*-a
Antonina Alekseyevna – Anton*ee*na Alek*say*evna
Begovaya – Bego*vaa*ya
Blok – Blawk
Dynamo – Dee*naam*o
Fandeyev – Fand*yay*ev
Golyshmanovo – Golysh*maan*ovo
Irina – Ee*ree*na
Kachalov – Ka*chaa*lov
Kalinkin – Ka*leen*kin

Khimki-Khovrino – *Kheem*ki-*Khawv*rino
Kovrigin – Kov*ree*gin
Luda – *Lyood*a
Malaya Gruzinskaya – *Maa*laya Gru*zeen*skaya
Malinkin – Ma*leen*kin
Mama – *Maam*a
Mamedov – Mamy*yed*ov
Mandelshtam – Mandel*shtaam*
Markushevich – Marku*shay*vich
Marya Petrovna – *Maar*ya Petra*wv*na
Nagatino – Na*gaat*ino
Nelda – *Nyel*da
Nevyadomsky – Ne*vyad*omsky
Novoslobodskaya – No-vo-slo-*bod*-ska-ya
Papa – *Paap*a
Pasternak – Paster*naak*
Pavlinovo – Pav*leen*ovo
Plekhanov – Ple*khaan*ov
Profsoyuznaya – Profso*yooz*naya
Prusakov – Proossa*kawf*
Sergei – Ser*gay*
Serpukhovka – Serpu*khawv*ka
Stepan – Ste*paan*
Taganka – Ta*gaan*ka
Tolstoy – Tol*stoy*
Tovt – Tawft
Tsvetayeva – Tsve-*tie*-yevna
Tsvetnoy – Tsvyet*noy*
Tyagusov – Tya*goos*ov
Vakhtangov – Vakh*taang*ov
Valya – *Vaal*ya
Vera Zasulich – *Vyer*a Zasoo*l*ich
Vernadsky – Ver*naad*sky

*Further titles in the
Methuen Modern Plays series
are listed overleaf.*